TAKE CONTROL OF YOUR TAX DEBT

TESTED TOOLS TO TACKLE YOUR IRS TAB

by

Robert C. Platt, Esq., JD, LLM

Library of Congress Control Number: 202491724

Book Cover by Laeek Hussain Arif

First Edition, August 2024

ISBN: 979-8-9911116-0-7

Dedicated to the American Taxpayer

"In this world, nothing can be said to be certain, except death, taxes, and the persistence of the IRS in collecting what is owed."

Preface

Hello, and thank you for taking a look at my book on IRS collections. My name is Robert Platt. I have been a practicing tax lawyer for over 30 years. Following law school, I completed a master's degree in tax law (LLM). For seven years, I taught federal tax law to law school students and have testified as an expert witness concerning complex federal tax-related matters. Most importantly, I have helped countless clients resolve their tax debt.

I have seen firsthand the stress and anxiety that tax debt can cause. Most people need help understanding the IRS collection process and are often unsure of what steps they should take to resolve their tax issues. Addressing these issues is unpleasant, and many of my clients had put off taking care of their tax troubles. Most sought help only after a jarring collection event. The most common event was the client discovering, without notice, that the IRS had seized all the money in their bank account. It does not have to be this way. By reading this book, you are taking the first step. You can do what I tell my clients: **take action now!**

I wrote this book to provide taxpayers with a clear explanation of the IRS collection system and their options for resolving their tax debt. This book will give you the tools to take action and put your tax debt behind you. While enlisting the aid of a tax professional is often advisable, there are situations where this may not be practical. Nonetheless, the information in this book is valuable to all taxpayers, regardless of whether they choose to seek professional assistance.

This book is for individuals who owe money to the IRS. It focuses exclusively on post-planning issues that arise after your case has reached the hands of the Internal Revenue Service collections function—the most formidable debt collector in the world.

In my experience, people expect the worst. They fear losing all of their money, and many think they will be left homeless. Believe it or not, that's not how the IRS works. Using the tools contained in this book, most of my clients have been pleasantly surprised with the terms of their resolution.

Important Author's Note

In the upcoming chapters, I will guide you through the various stages of the IRS collection process. From the first notice of tax due to the final resolution of your tax debt, we will delve into how the IRS manages unpaid taxes. Most importantly, we will explore the array of options available to you to resolve your tax debt. One or more of these options should work for you.

There are four parts to this book. Part I discusses general collection issues. This part will give you an overview of how the assessment and collections process works and what you can expect from the IRS if you owe them money. Part II discusses specific resolution options. Part III is titled Special Circumstances. This part delves into the various enforced collection actions the IRS may take and how you can respond to each. It also contains some statutory defenses you can use and explains how the collections statute of limitations may apply to you. Part IV includes some helpful information and resources for your review.

I understand that you might be tempted to skip to the part of the book that seems to address your particular issue. However, I recommend reading the first chapter, "Assessment and Collection Overview." This chapter provides essential information to help you understand the rest of the book. Once you have read the first chapter, you can proceed to the chapter dealing with your specific concern. Additionally, I have included endnotes that will direct you to more detailed information if you are interested.

The endnotes primarily refer to the following authorities:

- The Internal Revenue Code refers to Title 26 of the United States Code. The Internal Revenue Code contains the laws passed by Congress regarding all federal tax laws.

- The Internal Revenue Manual is a collection of internal guidelines for Internal Revenue Service employees. The manual contains instructions, procedures, and policies for the operation of all Internal Revenue Service organizations. It is not the law but an essential resource for understanding IRS policies and procedures. It tells us what to expect from the IRS in any given circumstance. The Internal Revenue Manual can be found online at **www.IRS.GOV/IRM**.

- Treasury Regulations are the highest administrative authority issued by the Treasury Department (of which the Internal Revenue Service is a part). Treasury Regulations are cited as "C.F.R." for "Code of Federal Regulations" or, alternatively as "Treas. Reg." which stands for Treasury Regulation. For example, the Treasury Regulations for Internal Revenue Code Section 6326 (administrative appeal of liens) will be cited as 26 C.F.R. § 301.6326-1 or Treas. Reg. § 301.6326-1.

- A Revenue Procedure ("Rev. Proc.") is an official statement of a procedure relating to the Internal Revenue Code, related statutes, or regulations that affect the rights or duties of taxpayers.

- A Revenue Ruling ("Rev. Rul.") is an official interpretation of the Internal Revenue Code, statutes, and regulations issued by the IRS. These rulings provide useful guidelines for taxpayers.

- References to tax cases decided in court are made in a standard case citation format. An internet search using the case citation will take you to the text of the decision.

Tax laws, regulations, and IRS policies are subject to change. While every effort has been made to ensure the accuracy and completeness of the information provided, there may be changes or updates that are not reflected in this book or that have occurred after the date of publication. If you are facing a critical issue or timing concern, it is best to consult with a tax professional. If you are unable to do so, verify the requirements with the IRS or by referencing the applicable statute, regulation, or policy. The author and publisher disclaim any liability for any loss or damage incurred as a result of the use of the information contained in this book.

Table of Contents

PART I: OVERVIEW

CHAPTER 1:

Assessment and Collection Overview

Please take a moment to familiarize yourself with the following tax-specific terms and concepts. They will enhance the coherence of the remaining chapters.

IRS Forms

Nearly every interaction with the IRS requires the use of purpose-designed IRS forms. These forms offer the advantage of uniformity, ensuring that all necessary information is provided when completed correctly. Designed with taxpayers in mind, they do not typically require specialized legal knowledge to fill out. While most forms are self-explanatory, accompanying instructions are available to guide you through the process. This book references specific forms necessary for various actions and, where applicable, provides additional guidance on completing potentially challenging sections of the forms. Most chapters conclude with a list of related forms and IRS publications that may assist you further. Forms can be accessed directly on **IRS.gov** by entering the form number (preceded by the word "form") in the search box. Most forms can be completed online and printed from your home computer.

Assessment of Tax

Assessment occurs when you have filed your tax return, and the IRS enters the amount of tax you owe on the official assessment roll. Assessment can also occur when the IRS audits you and finds you owe more money or if the IRS files a return for you after you have neglected to file one. If you file a tax return with an amount due, it is said to be self-assessed.

Substitute for Return

If you haven't filed your tax return for several years, the IRS has a tool to file one for you. It is called a "Substitute for Return" (SFR). The IRS will prepare an SFR using the information it has about you, including wages and other income you have received during the year. You will usually owe less tax if you file your own return because only you know what deductions and credits are available in your case.

Notice of Tax Due and Demand for Payment

This is the first notice you receive when you officially owe money to the IRS. The Notice of Tax Due and Demand for Payment starts the collection process.

Notice of Intent to Levy

The IRS is legally required to send you a Notice of Intent to Levy before they seize your property.[1] This document will also explain your appeal rights and the time frame within which you can appeal.

Notice of Federal Tax Lien

A Federal Tax Lien is a legal claim against all of your current and future property. A Federal Tax Lien arises as a matter of law if you don't pay your liability when you receive the Notice of Tax Due and Demand for Payment. The lien becomes public notice when the IRS files a Notice of Federal Tax Lien. Once the IRS files the Notice of Federal Tax Lien, you may have problems obtaining credit, refinancing, or selling your property.

Levy (Seizure)

A levy occurs when the IRS takes your money or property to satisfy your tax debt. The most common example of a levy is when the IRS seizes the money in your bank account. The IRS can also seize your wages by using a wage garnishment. If the IRS seizes non-monetary property, they will sell it and apply the proceeds to your debt.

Appeal

You can appeal most actions or proposed actions to the Independent Office of Appeals. The Independent Office of Appeals (often called "Appeals") is an independent organization within the IRS. They help resolve certain tax disputes in an informal, administrative process. Many times, this appeal can take place via correspondence or telephone meetings. Don't let the fact that Appeals is part of the IRS dissuade you from using their services. My experience is that Appeals will treat you fairly and, in most cases, assist in resolving your issue.

United States Tax Court

In some cases, the Tax Court will have jurisdiction to review disputes, assess the accuracy of an IRS action or to address an appeal if you disagree with the decision made by Appeals. The Tax Court has limited jurisdiction, and you must adhere to strict time periods. If you need to petition the Tax Court, it is best to consult with a tax attorney.

Taxpayer Advocate Service

The IRS is a large bureaucracy. Due to the sheer volume of cases, sometimes a taxpayer will experience an undue delay or face other issues while trying to resolve their matter. If you cannot resolve your issue through the usual channels, and this results in an undue hardship, you can seek assistance from the Taxpayer Advocate Service. As with the Office of Appeals, the Taxpayer Advocate Service is an independent organization within the IRS. I have found the Taxpayer Advocate Service to be very helpful, professional, and able to cut through red tape to resolve cases when the normal channels are not working correctly or as fast as they should.

Collection Statute Expiration Date ("CSED")

Contrary to popular belief, the IRS will eventually stop attempting to collect money from you. The Internal Revenue Code gives the IRS ten years from the date of assessment to collect your tax.[2] The CSED is important for three reasons. First, the IRS determines what payment plans can be used based on the CSED.

Second, you may engage in activities (such as appeals) that will extend the CSED. And third, you may be relieved of some of your older liabilities if this date passes. If you want to know what your CSED is, just call the IRS and ask. They track the CSED for each of your tax years.

Delinquent Return Filing Requirement

Most tax resolutions require that the taxpayer be current with his or her filing requirements. The IRS, however, pursuant to IRS Policy Statement 5-133,[3] typically enforces the filing of delinquent returns for the last six years. This means, for example, if you have not filed for the last eight years, the IRS is likely to only require you to file the most recent six years. If the IRS is going to enforce more years (or if they propose to enforce fewer years) managerial approval will be required.

COLLECTION LIFECYCLE

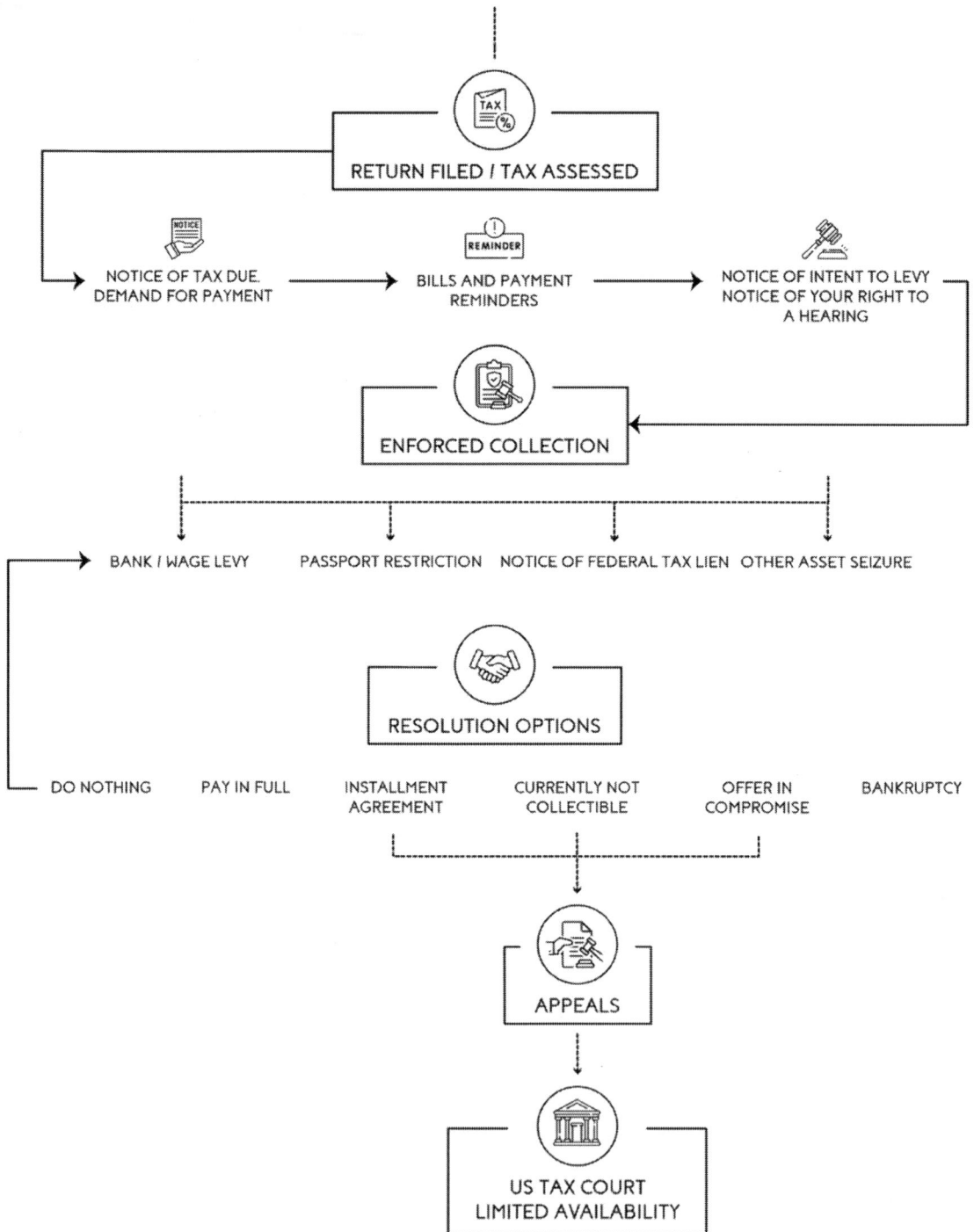

RETURN FILED / TAX ASSESSED

NOTICE OF TAX DUE.
DEMAND FOR PAYMENT → BILLS AND PAYMENT
REMINDERS → NOTICE OF INTENT TO LEVY
NOTICE OF YOUR RIGHT TO
A HEARING

ENFORCED COLLECTION

BANK / WAGE LEVY   PASSPORT RESTRICTION   NOTICE OF FEDERAL TAX LIEN   OTHER ASSET SEIZURE

RESOLUTION OPTIONS

DO NOTHING   PAY IN FULL   INSTALLMENT
AGREEMENT   CURRENTLY NOT
COLLECTIBLE   OFFER IN
COMPROMISE   BANKRUPTCY

APPEALS

**US TAX COURT
LIMITED AVAILABILITY**

Lifecycle of a Collection Case

This book addresses, in detail, the various collection alternatives available for the individual taxpayer. However, to get a big picture of how the collection system works, here is the lifecycle of the typical collection case.

Stage One – Assessment of Tax

You self-assess taxes by filing your tax return. Occasionally, an audit will result in the assessment of additional tax. Once a tax is "assessed" it is considered legally owed.

If you have not filed returns for several years, the IRS will send notices requesting you file them. If you ignore these notices, the IRS will file a return for you. This IRS-filed return is called a Substitute for Return (SFR). After the IRS prepares the SFR and notifies you, you will have a specific period of time to contest the amount owed. Once that time has lapsed, the IRS will assess the tax and start sending bills for the assessed amount.

Sometimes, the IRS acts slowly, which might give you a false sense of security, as if the IRS has forgotten about you. Trust me, they haven't.

Stage Two – Notices to Taxpayer

The IRS will send you bills once the tax is assessed. The letters start benignly, reminding you of the amount due and requesting payment. Then, the letters get progressively harsher until a Final Notice of Intent to Levy and Notice of Your Right to a Hearing is issued. This notice (unless hand delivered) is mailed via certified mail to your last known address. You do not have to receive the letter; the law just requires that it be properly mailed. If you have a certified letter awaiting you at the post office, go get it. There is no advantage to ignoring the letter.

This Notice of Intent to Levy will inform you that the IRS may levy your assets in 30 days if there is no resolution of your tax matter before then. My experience is that it takes a bit more time for them to levy, but not much. It is best practice to resolve the issue long before the expiration of the 30-day deadline. Also, if this notice gives you appeal rights, you should complete and submit the form to appeal the proposed levy unless you immediately resolve the case with the IRS.

Stage Three – Enforced Collection

It is best to take action during Stage One or Stage Two, but not everybody does. If you don't, the next stage includes enforced collection. Enforced collection is collection action without your consent. Remember, your financial institutions and employer report your income to the IRS at least annually. The IRS knows where you keep your money if it is in the financial system. In this stage, the IRS will levy your bank accounts, seizing the entire balance up to the amount of your tax bill. The IRS will levy (or garnish) your wages by contacting your employer and ordering your employer to send your paycheck to the IRS. There is a small exempt amount, but your employer is required to remit most of the check to the IRS. The IRS may levy your investment accounts, social security benefits, and state tax refunds. In some cases, the IRS will forward your case to the State Department, which will revoke your passport if you have a high enough balance.

The IRS knows it might not collect all the tax due using these methods, but it is guaranteed to get your attention. Most people cannot survive financially if their bank balances and paychecks are seized. Once the IRS has your attention, you need to take action to request a resolution of your case.

Stage Four – Resolution Alternatives

If you owe the IRS money, you will have the following options:

- Do nothing. This option is generally short-lived because the IRS will end up taking your money. If you ignore the IRS, they will continue to seize assets.
- Pay in Full. Although not an option for everybody, paying in full will reduce interest and penalties and relieve you from dealing with the IRS. If you are reading this book, however, it is likely that immediate full payment is not an option.
- Installment Agreement. The IRS will agree to an Installment Agreement consisting of a monthly payment. The most the IRS will demand as a monthly payment is the difference between your monthly gross income and your monthly necessary living expenses. However, it is more common to negotiate a smaller payment based upon one of the many Installment Agreement programs.

- Currently Not Collectible. A Currently Not Collectible status exists when you only have enough income to meet basic living expenses. If this is the case, the IRS will defer collection until a later date.

- Offer in Compromise. When you cannot pay your taxes within the collection period (generally ten years from the assessment date), the IRS may accept a lesser amount to satisfy the debt.

- Bankruptcy. This option does not work for newer tax debts but may be suitable in cases where other options are ineffective or less beneficial.

Stage Five - Appeals

Most of the time, you can resolve your debt using one of the above alternatives. However, in some cases, the IRS will take action or propose to take action that you do not agree with. In these cases, you can appeal the determinations of the collection representative using one of the available appeal options. In most cases, The Independent Office of Appeals will hear and decide disputes between you and the IRS. This will be discussed in detail later in this book. In limited circumstances, you can petition the Tax Court if you do not agree with the decision by Appeals.

Who You Will Be Talking To

Depending on the specifics of your case, you will be interacting with one of three groups within the collection function:

Automated Collection System

Also known as "ACS," this is the department with which the vast majority of taxpayers interact. ACS is a computerized inventory system and telephone call center. They issue the letters and can file notices of federal tax lien or issue levies. When you owe money and call the IRS, these are the people you will be speaking with. The representatives can be a big help, but your case will not be assigned to a specific representative. If you do not resolve your issue on the first call, you will speak to a different representative when you call back. Each representative, however, has access to your account and the notes left by representatives you have spoken to previously.

Field Collections

This function is for large balance cases or cases involving payroll taxes (the IRS takes payroll tax cases very seriously). The representatives who work in Field Collections are called revenue officers. They are specially trained collectors. Your resolution options are the same as those with ACS and Field Collections. However, if you are dealing with a revenue officer, you will find they are a bit stricter and impose tighter timelines than those at ACS. As a general rule, revenue officers will only visit your home or place of work if they let you know ahead of time. If a revenue officer wants to meet with you in person, they will send an appointment letter (Letter 725-B). In only the most extreme cases will you receive an unannounced visit. An unannounced visit typically occurs only in cases where asset seizure is necessary because the assets are at risk of being moved beyond the IRS's reach. An unannounced visit may also occur for service of a subpoena or summons. If an agent visits you, you can ask for their official identification. You should ask to see their IRS-issued credential (also called a "pocket commission") and their HSPD-12 Card.[4] These credentials include a serial number and an agent's photograph. If you have doubts about their legitimacy, you can take down their name and ID number and call the IRS at their general number, 800-829-1040, to confirm the legitimacy of the representative.

Private Collection Agencies

The IRS works with private collection agencies to assist in collecting certain overdue tax debts. At the time of this writing, the private collection agencies used by the IRS are CBE Group Inc. of Waterloo, IA; Coast Professional, Inc. of Geneseo, NY; and ConServe of Fairport, NY. These agencies are assigned older tax debts, when the IRS is too busy and your case is too small for them to pursue. If your case is assigned to a private collection agency, the IRS will send you a CP40 Notice. This notice informs you that your case has been assigned to a private collection agency, and will explain the process. The private collection agency will also send you a letter with a request that you call. The letter will contain an authorization code for you to use to authenticate your account. If you want to ensure they are legitimate, call the IRS at 800-829-1040 and ask. They will be able to confirm if your case has been assigned to the private collection agency. It is important to note that these agencies do not have any enforced collection authority. They cannot issue levies or file notices of federal tax lien. Neither can they settle your tax bill due to hardship. Because you won't have the full range of options with the private collection agency, I recommend you have your file transferred back to the IRS if you are interested in entering into an Installment Agreement, pursuing a Currently Not Collectible status or submitting an Offer in Compromise. You will need to request the transfer of your account in a letter to the agency. To do so, simply mail a letter to the return address along with a copy of the notice they mailed to you. In the body of the letter, write, "Please return my file to the IRS." The transfer process will take a couple of months. I have had clients who were waiting for the CSED to expire and have just ignored the private collection agency and let the clock tick.

IMPORTANT WARNING

Do not fall for a scam!

- The IRS will not call you first. They will send you letters via the United States Postal Service. You will never receive a call from a random agent without first receiving notices from the IRS.
- The IRS will not email you.
- The IRS will not text you.
- The IRS will not contact you via any social media account.
- The IRS will not leave you a pre-recorded voicemail.
- The IRS will not ask for a credit card number (or for gift cards).
- A real IRS agent will understand your need to verify their legitimacy.

Unless you are sure the communication you receive is legitimate, call the known IRS number (800-829-1040). They can look up your account and determine if it has been assigned to an individual revenue officer.

IRS Forms and Publications Related to This Chapter:

- *Publication 594 – The IRS Collection Process*

CHAPTER 2:

It All Starts with the Assessment

In the United States, the income tax system is primarily based on self-assessment. You file your tax return, typically by April 15, reporting your income, claiming deductions and credits, and calculating your tax liability. The tax becomes officially due when the IRS enters this amount on the assessment rolls. If your entire tax liability has not been paid with the tax return or through withholding or estimated tax payments, the collection process will automatically begin.

In addition to self-assessment, there are two less common scenarios. The first occurs if you have been audited and the IRS finds that you owe additional tax. In this case, the IRS will send you an examination report that shows how the additional tax was determined. You can agree to the findings and consent in writing to the assessment. You can also contest the findings through the appeals process and ultimately to the US Tax Court. If you do not prevail, the taxes will be assessed. If you ignore the IRS, they will send you a Notice of Deficiency. If you fail to petition the Tax Court within the prescribed time, the assessment will become final and the collection efforts will begin.

The second scenario is called a Substitute for Return (SFR). The IRS receives third-party reporting documents (e.g. W-2 and 1099) annually. The IRS matches these forms against your tax returns. If you fail to file, the IRS will refer to these reporting documents to file a tax return on your behalf. They usually send you notices requesting that you file your returns. If you ignore the notices, the IRS will file your tax return for you. They will include all of your income but will not give you any deductions or credits resulting in a higher tax liability that if you had properly filed your own return. The IRS will then follow the same procedure as they do in an audit, giving you the opportunity to object and petition the Tax Court. If you fail to do so, the assessment will become final. It usually takes a few years for the IRS to file a SFR for you.

No matter the mechanism for assessment, the result is the same - you owe money to the IRS.

But that's not all. In most circumstances, the IRS will assess penalties. Common penalties include the following:

- Failure to file on time.

- Failure to pay the amount of tax due.

- Failure to make adequate estimated payments or have adequate taxes withheld from the taxpayer's wages.

- If the assessment resulted from an audit, there may be penalties for making errors on the original tax return.

Finally, interest charges will accrue if you do not pay the IRS promptly.

CHAPTER 3:

Can You Represent Yourself?

You can represent yourself before the IRS. In some cases, the issues are simple, but in my experience, most people just don't want to deal with the IRS. It can be intimidating, and many clients just hand over the case and say, "Please just deal with it for me." It is best to have an experienced advocate, but that is not always a choice.

You can contact, negotiate, and resolve matters regarding your case. However, you also have the right to representation before the IRS by the following individuals:

- Attorney at law.
- Certified Public Accountant (CPA).
- Enrolled Agent (EA). These individuals have taken a test to qualify to practice before the IRS.
- Low-Income Taxpayer Clinic Student Intern. With specific approval by the IRS, these interns may practice before the IRS.
- Unenrolled Return Preparer. A preparer of your return has limited representation rights before the IRS.
- Your immediate family member. An immediate family member includes a spouse, child, parent, brother, or sister.
- An officer of a corporation can represent the corporation.
- A regular full-time employee can represent his or her employer.
- A fiduciary, such as a trustee, executor, guardian, etc., stands in the taxpayer's position. In some cases, a fiduciary does not need a power of attorney.

Form 2848, Power of Attorney and Declaration of Representative is used to appoint another person as your representative for tax purposes. Have this form signed and ready to fax when your representative first calls the IRS. The representative must fax it in to speak with the IRS about your account. Alternatively, the representative can electronically submit or mail the form to the IRS. However, the IRS must process the form before speaking with your representative. It can take up to two or three weeks for the IRS to process these forms.

Form 8821 Tax Information Authorization allows your designated party to inspect and/or receive confidential tax information from the IRS, including tax returns. This form does not authorize the designated party to act on behalf of or represent you.

Tax Tip: The forms are easy to complete, and most details address the taxpayer's and representative's identity and contact information. However, when completing the field for "Years or Periods," do not enter "all years" or "all periods." The IRS will not process the power of attorney if you use such language. You can enter each year or period or list consecutive periods, such as "2015 thru 2024." The ending period cannot be over three years in the future.

IRS Forms and Publications Related to This Chapter:

- *Form 2848 – Power of Attorney (and instructions for this form)*
- *Form 8821 – Tax Information Authorization (and instructions for this form)*

CHAPTER 4:

Collection Begins as Soon as You Owe the Tax

Once the IRS has sent a bill that is left unpaid, the collection efforts begin with a series of ever harsher letters. The letters are generally sent in this order, though sometimes the IRS may skip a step or two:[5]

- CP14, Non-Math Error Balance Due
- CP501, 1st Notice – Balance Due
- CP503, 2nd Notice – Balance Due
- CP504, Final Notice – Balance Due
- LT11, Final Notice, Notice of Intent to Levy and Notice of Your Right to a Hearing
- LT1058, Final Notice, Notice of Intent to Levy and Notice of Your Right to a Hearing

If those letters are unanswered, the IRS will throw a host of collection tools at you, including:

- Filing of Notice of Federal Tax Lien.
- Wage garnishment (seizure).
- Bank Levies (seizure of bank account balances).
- Levies of investment accounts.
- Levies of personal property, e.g., cars, boats, artwork, etc.
- Seizure of accounts receivable or amounts others owe you.
- Revocation of your passport, thus restricting your right to travel outside the country.

When you owe additional taxes, the IRS will send a letter entitled "Notice of Tax Due and Demand for Payment" to your last known address. The notice provides detailed information about the amount owed, the tax period in question, and the deadline for payment.[6]

If you ignore the Notice of Tax Due and Demand for Payment, the IRS will send several reminder letters, each more forceful than the last. The final letter in the series is a "Notice of Intent to Levy and Notice of Your Right to a Hearing." By law, the IRS must mail this notice via certified mail to your last known address.[7] You don't need to receive the letter; it just has to be mailed via Certified Mail. The notice gives you 30 days to pay the tax bill or make other arrangements with the IRS. This notice includes information regarding your appeal rights. Under most circumstances, you can appeal the proposed levy by filing a Collection Due Process Appeal within 30 days of the date the notice was issued.

Unless you take action, the IRS will begin "enforced collection." Although they can start this process after 30 days, they usually allow a bit more time. Waiting beyond the 30 days is risky, though. If you owe money and the IRS has started this process, it is best not to wait any longer. Call the IRS.

Bank Account Levies

If you do not respond to the IRS, they usually start their enforced collection by seizing assets held by third parties. This is easier for the IRS and reduces the risk of confrontation. Consequently, enforced collection usually begins with a levy on your bank account. The IRS has a record of your bank accounts because the bank accounts report interest income annually to the IRS. The IRS will contact the bank and seize all the money in the account.[8] Aside from the initial Notice of Intent to Levy, there will be no notice of the levy until they have blocked your access to the funds. Once the bank receives the notice of levy against the account, it must hold the funds for 21 calendar days to allow you to appeal the action. After 21 days, unless released by the IRS, the bank will remit the funds to the IRS. Although there are circumstances in which the IRS will release the levy, it is my experience that once they have control of the money, the IRS is reluctant to release it. This will be discussed later in detail.

Seizure of Wages

In addition to bank levies, the IRS may garnish (seize) your wages. Like banks, your employer reports your income to the IRS annually, so the IRS likely knows where you work. The IRS has the authority to seize almost all of your paycheck.

These are attention-getting actions. Although these actions net the IRS some past-due funds, their goal is to bring you to the table and resolve the debt using one of the options outlined later in this book.

Seizure of a Portion of Your Social Security Benefits

The IRS can seize up to 15% of your social security benefits.[9]

Seizure of Your State/Municipal Tax Refund

The IRS has agreements with some states and municipalities to seize your state or local refund and apply it to your federal tax debt. Under the State Income Tax Levy Program, the IRS matches federal tax delinquent accounts against a database of state tax refunds for states participating in the State Income Tax Levy Program. If your refund has been seized, you will be notified by the state and by the IRS. The IRS will allow you to appeal. There is a similar arrangement with municipalities under the Municipal Tax Levy Program and the State of Alaska where the IRS can seize your Permanent Fund Dividend.

Other Asset Seizures

The IRS has more collection tools that are less frequently employed but are available as the case may dictate. These include the seizure of your house, car, retirement account, and any other property you own or in which you have an interest.

Federal Tax Liens

The IRS has yet more tools. Under certain circumstances, the IRS will file a Notice of Federal Tax lien in your county of residence and other counties in which you are known to own real estate. The filed Notice of Federal Tax Lien will, subject to some limitations, eliminate your ability to sell or refinance your real property without first paying the IRS debt.

Passport Restrictions

The IRS also has a relatively new collection tool. As of 2015, if the total tax, penalties, and interest exceeds $62,000,[10] the IRS may notify the State Department, which can revoke or refuse to renew your passport.

The IRS's goal is voluntary compliance, and it uses its increasingly severe methods only when you ignore them.

IRS Forms and Publications Related to This Chapter:

- *Publication 594 – The IRS Collection Process*

PART II: SOLUTIONS

CHAPTER 5:

Your Call to the IRS

The IRS phone number is 800-829-1040, 7:00 a.m. to 7:00 p.m. local time.

You will find it easier to negotiate with the IRS if you are current on filing your returns and have proper tax withholding from your paychecks (or paying estimated tax if you are self-employed). If you are not in compliance, do not let this delay your call to the IRS. Most of the time, they will give you time to comply.

Although you can take care of some items online, in my experience, you will get the best treatment by speaking with a representative live on the telephone. During my first contact with my clients, most told me they dreaded calling the IRS and had put it off until the last minute. Don't dread it. Do it. I will tell you what to expect.

It is essential to know a couple of things to set the stage. The person you talk to takes dozens of calls daily, dealing with the same issues. They have no skin in the game. Unlike private litigation, such as a personal lawsuit, the representative you speak with just wants to get through his or her day. They don't get a bonus for squeezing more money out of you. If your case fits neatly within one of their boxes, they are just as comfortable placing you in a Currently Not Collectible status (where collection actions against you are suspended, i.e., you need not make payments) as they are signing you up for a hefty Installment Agreement. If you take the proper tone with the representative, you will usually be surprised at how helpful they can be. The representatives are on the receiving end of angry taxpayers all day long. When I speak with the IRS, in every case, I approach it as follows: "Good Morning, my client has found himself in a real pickle, and I'm hoping you can help me out." Clients who take this approach rather than the angry one fare better simply due to human nature.

Every once in a while, I run into a representative who is hostile and unhelpful. It doesn't happen often, but it does happen. When that happens, I politely state that I have an urgent issue to attend to and will call back. Because of the sheer volume of calls, a different representative will answer upon my callback. That will solve the problem of having to deal with a cranky representative.

Who to Call

If you receive a notice, a callback number will be listed. Use that number. If you don't have a notice, you can call the main IRS number at 1-800-829-1040. They take calls from 7:00 a.m. to 7:00 p.m. local time. Your call is routed by caller ID so that local time will mean the local time of the geographic area covered by your area code. Even though I am in the Mountain Time Zone, I have an East Coast area code. Therefore, I am routed to the East Coast and must adjust my calling times accordingly.

When to Call

Sometimes, the wait times are a challenge. Your best bet is to avoid calling Monday morning and Friday afternoon, as those will have the highest call volumes. In my experience, calling at 7:00 a.m. Tuesday through Thursday will get your call answered fastest.

What to Expect

You will have a couple of screening prompts and then be asked to enter your social security number. After (hopefully) a short time of listening to elevator music, a representative will come on the line. They will ask what they can help you with. Don't go into details yet; they are just ensuring you are in the right place. You can respond with something like, *"I'm calling because I owe money from my 2020 tax return. I cannot pay it, and I hope you can help me."*

Next, the IRS representative will ask several questions to confirm your identity. They will ask your name as it appears on your tax return, address, and social security number and ask another question or two to verify it is you. Some of the questions they may ask include:

- Your date of birth.

- Your filing status (single, married, filing jointly, etc.).
- The number of dependents reported on your return.

Once they confirm it is you, they will verify your contact information. They might also ask questions to identify "levy sources." These are sources they can levy, such as your current employer or bank account. Their policy directs them to ask these questions. Although providing them with levy sources may be unsettling, know that as long as you are working with them, they will not levy. It is OK to give them this information. They likely have this information already. After all of this, they will ask how they can help.

The most common call to the IRS is to set up a payment plan. If this is the case, you would ask, *"I would like to set up a payment plan for the money I owe for 2020."* The first question they will ask is, *"Can you pay the full amount or borrow money to pay the full amount now or in the near future?"* If you can't, tell them you can't. They will then ask, "How much do you think you can pay monthly?" It is advisable to maintain some financial flexibility. Start low. Ask, *"What is the smallest amount I would be allowed to pay in an Installment Agreement?"* At that point, the representative will determine which Installment Agreement plan (outlined below) you would qualify for. Initially, the representative will give you a monthly payment based on a streamlined Installment Agreement (see balance requirements in the Installment Agreement Chapter). This plan pays the balance over six years in most cases. This number will work for most people due to the longer payment period. If this amount is too much for you, you can tell the representative, *"I'm sorry, with my current financial circumstances, I just cannot pay that."*

In that case, the representative will ask you to provide them with some numbers from your *Form 433-F, Collection Information Statement.* They can usually take this information over the phone and don't require you to submit the document. It is best to have this information ready when you make your first call. Based on your unique financial circumstances, the representative will devise a monthly payment amount based on your balance, monthly income and expenses and the remaining time the IRS has to legally collect your debt (see Collection Statute Expiration Date later in this book).

The IRS will usually be flexible if you need time to consider the options or gather more information. I typically receive ten days to two weeks when I need more time during an interaction with the collection representatives. Since your case is in collections, you don't want any surprises, such as a levy, while you are working on your case. Therefore, you should ask the representative to place a "hold" on collections while you are working on it. It will sound like this, *"Thank you for your help; I'm concerned about a seizure of my bank account or a wage garnishment. Can I please have a hold placed on collection activities while I [whatever you need to do]?"* They will usually agree to a hold and will tell you how long. A 30 or 45-day hold is not uncommon. Make sure you follow up.

If the IRS has already taken enforcement steps, such as seizing the funds in your bank account, see the tips listed in the following chapters.

CHAPTER 6:

Getting the Numbers Right

In the last chapter, you learned what to expect from the IRS when they try to collect your debt. However, it is easy to short-circuit their collection protocol. Contact the IRS and initiate a discussion regarding how you can address your debt.

In the meantime, you will want to ensure you only pay what you owe. There are a few cases where a downward adjustment in your tax bill is possible.

IRS Math Error

It is rare for the IRS to make a math error, but it does occur. Perhaps payments have been made to the IRS that are not credited to the proper account. Double-check your records and your payment against any IRS correspondence you receive or against your transcript if you have ordered one. The IRS will also review your account with you on the telephone. That is the easiest and quickest way to resolve any discrepancy between your figures and the IRS figures.

Substitute for Return

Another opportunity to reduce your balance is in the case where the IRS has filed a "Substitute for Return" (called an SFR by the IRS). If you fail to file a tax return, the Internal Revenue Service may take matters into its own hands and file a tax return on your behalf. The IRS's process for filing a Substitute for Return is as follows:

1. If you are obligated to file a return and have not done so, the IRS will prepare the SFR using the information in its file. Every year the IRS gets copies of all of your tax forms (forms W-2, 1099, 1098, etc.). The IRS uses the figures from these forms to file your tax return for you.

2. The IRS calculates tax liability based on the income information in its file. However, the SFR does not consider any deductions or credits that you may be entitled to claim. As a result, the amount of tax owed on the SFR is often higher than your correct tax liability.

3. Once the IRS prepares the SFR, they will send a letter explaining the proposed tax liability and giving you notice that you have 30 days to explain why you are not required to file a return, submit a completed tax return, or consent to the assessment.

4. If you do not respond to the letter from the IRS, the IRS will issue a Statutory Notice of Deficiency showing the deficiency amount and giving you 90 days to petition the Tax Court. The assessment will become final if 90 days lapse without petitioning the Tax Court. At that point, collection efforts will commence.

5. Even if the IRS has completed all these steps, you can file a correct return with the reconsideration unit.[11] They will review the return and, if appropriate, adjust your account accordingly. Reducing your tax will also reduce the penalties and interest.

If the IRS has filed an SFR for you, filing a correct return with the IRS will likely reduce your liability. You will need to submit your return to a special address for reconsideration. Call the IRS at 800-829-1040. They will give you the correct address to mail the late tax return.

Transcripts

If you need to file a late tax return and don't have all your income records, you can request a "Wage and Income Transcript." This transcript will list the income on forms W-2, 1099, and related forms. This transcript may contain other helpful documents, such as mortgage interest paid. There are three ways to obtain these transcripts:

1. Call the IRS at 800-829-1040 and request the transcript.

2. Complete and mail a Form 4506-T, Request for Transcript of Tax Return.

3. If you have an online account, use the Get Transcript Online function.

For current information related to obtaining your transcript, you may visit **IRS.gov/individuals/get-transcript**

Tax Transcripts Options

The IRS will provide you, free of charge, with transcripts of data they have on record for your tax history. The types of tax transcripts are as follows:

1. **Tax Return Transcript** - shows most line items from your original Form 1040-series tax return as filed, along with any forms and schedules. It doesn't show changes made after you filed your original return. This transcript is available for the current and three prior tax years. A tax return transcript usually meets the needs of lending institutions offering mortgages. Note: The secondary spouse on a joint return can use Get Transcript Online or *Form 4506-T, Request for Transcript of Tax Return* to request this transcript type. When using Get Transcript by Mail or calling 800-908-9946, the primary taxpayer on the return must make the request.

2. **Tax Account Transcript** - shows basic data such as filing status, taxable income, and payment types. It also shows changes made after you filed your original return. This transcript is available for the current and nine prior tax years through Get Transcript Online and the current and three prior tax years through Get Transcript by Mail or by calling 800-908-9946. These years and older tax years can be obtained by submitting *Form 4506-T, Request for Transcript of Tax Return*. Note: If you made estimated tax payments and/or applied an overpayment from a prior year's return, you can request this transcript type a few weeks after the beginning of the calendar year to confirm your payments before filing your tax return.

3. **Record of Account Transcript** - This transcript combines the tax return and tax account transcripts above into one complete transcript. It is available for the current and three prior tax years using Get Transcript Online or *Form 4506-T, Request for Transcript of Tax Retu*m.

4. **Wage and Income Transcript** - shows data from information returns received by the IRS, such as *Forms W-2* (Wage and Tax Statement), *1098* (Mortgage Interest Statement), *1099* (shows different types of income other than wages), and *5498* (IRA Contribution Statement). The transcript is limited to approximately 85 income documents. If you have more documents than that, the transcript will

not generate. You'll receive a notification online stating that your transcript request cannot be processed and that you must complete and submit *Form 4506-T, Request for Transcript of Tax Return*. If you see a message saying "No Record of return filed" for the current tax year, it means information has not yet been populated in the transcript. Check back in late May. This transcript is available for the current and nine prior tax years using Get Transcript Online or *Form 4506-T, Request for Transcript of Tax Return*.

5. **Verification of Non-filing Letter** - states that the IRS has no record of a processed Form 1040-series tax return as of the date of the request. It doesn't indicate whether you are required to file a return for that year. This letter is available after June 15 for the current tax year or anytime for the prior three tax years using Get Transcript Online or *Form 4506-T, Request for Transcript of Tax Return*. Use Form *4506-T, Request for Transcript of Tax Return* if you need a letter for older tax years.

Note: A transcript isn't a photocopy of your return. If you need a copy of your original return, *submit Form 4506, Request for Copy of Tax Return*. The processing time and fee are listed on the form.

Steps to Take if an SFR May Have Been Filed

- Call the IRS at the number on your notice or 800-829-1040.
- Request a year-by-year breakdown of your liabilities.
- Ask if any are the result of a Substitute for Return (SFR).
  - If so, ask for a Tax Account Transcript for that year. This will show the income the IRS used to complete the SFR.
- Ask for a breakdown of assessed penalties.
- Review your transcript and file a correct return, if applicable.

Penalty Abatement (Cancellation of Penalty)

Another potential method to reduce the amount you owe is to request a penalty abatement. You must file your tax returns on time and pay any taxes due by the deadline set by the IRS. Failure to file on time or pay on time will result in various penalties and interest charges. However, there may be situations where you have a reasonable cause for noncompliance. In such cases, you may request penalty abatement from the IRS.

Penalty abatement is a process that allows you to request relief from penalties assessed by the IRS. One avenue for penalty relief is "reasonable cause." This relief is available if you show that you used ordinary care and prudence to comply with tax obligations but could not comply due to circumstances beyond your control. Examples include noncompliance due to illness, natural disaster, or other unforeseen circumstances.

The two most common penalties for noncompliance are the *late filing penalty* and the *failure to pay penalty*. The IRS assesses a late filing penalty when you fail to file your tax returns by the due date, usually April 15th. The penalty is 5% of the unpaid taxes for each month or part of a month that the return is late, up to a maximum of 25% of the unpaid taxes.

The IRS will assess a "*failure to pay*" penalty when you do not pay the taxes owed by the due date. This penalty is 0.5% of the unpaid taxes for each month or part of a month that the tax remains unpaid, up to a maximum of 25% of the unpaid taxes.

If the IRS has assessed a penalty against you, consider requesting a penalty abatement if you believe you have reasonable cause for failing to comply with the payment or filing requirements. You can submit a written request for penalty abatement to the IRS using *Form 843, Claim for Refund and Request for Abatement.* In the request, you must explain the circumstances that led to the noncompliance and how those circumstances prevented you from meeting your tax obligations.

When arguing for penalty abatement, you can use several elements to increase the chances of a successful outcome. These elements include:

Reasonable Cause

When abating a penalty for reasonable cause, the IRS examines all facts and circumstances. Abatement is generally granted when you exercised ordinary business care and prudence in determining your tax obligations but were nevertheless unable to comply with those obligations.[12] The different types of reasonable cause are discussed below.

Ordinary Business Care and Prudence

Exercising ordinary business care and prudence includes making provisions for obligations to be met when reasonably foreseeable events occur. You may establish reasonable cause by providing facts and circumstances showing that you exercised ordinary business care and prudence (defined as taking that degree of care that a reasonably prudent person would exercise), but nevertheless were unable to comply with the law.[13] The IRS will review the following information:

- The dates and explanations must correspond with the events on which the penalties are based. For example, a medical emergency in 2025 would not correspond to a failure to file in 2023.

- Your compliance history will be examined for at least the three previous tax years. A first time penalty would be more likely to be abated than if you were assessed the same penalty year after year.[14]

- The IRS will examine the length of time it took you to comply following the removal of the impediment to compliance. The longer this period of time, the less likely the penalty will be abated.[15]

Death, Serious Illness, or Unavoidable Absence

Death, serious illness, or unavoidable absence of the taxpayer or death or serious illness in the taxpayer's immediate family may establish reasonable cause. Some of the factors the IRS will consider in these cases include:

- Your relationship to the other parties involved.

- The date of death or the dates, duration, and severity of the illness.

- Dates and reason for unavoidable absence, if applicable.

- How the event prevented your compliance.

- The degree to which other business obligations were impaired. If taxes were the only obligation that was impaired, it is less likely an abatement would be granted.

- If you addressed your tax obligations promptly when the event passed or within a reasonable time thereafter.

Fire, Casualty, Disaster, or Other Disturbance

In the event you were prevented from complying with tax obligations due to fire, casualty, natural disaster, or other disturbance despite the exercise of ordinary business care, abatement may be granted. Factors the IRS will consider include:

- The timing of the event.
- The effect the event had on your business or how you were affected in such a way that prevented your compliance.
- Steps you took in an attempt to comply.

Inability to Obtain Records

If you were unable to obtain records necessary to comply with your tax obligations, abatement may be granted.[16] As with other reasonable cause abatements, you must establish that you exercised ordinary business care and prudence but were unable to comply due to circumstances beyond your control. When requesting abatement under this provision, the IRS will look at the following factors:

- Why the records were needed to comply with the tax laws.
- Steps you took to secure the records and why they were unavailable.
- When and how you discovered the unavailability of the records.
- If you explored alternative methods to obtain the records.
- If you contacted the IRS for instructions due to the missing information.
- If you promptly complied once the missing information was received.
- Supporting records, such as letters written and responses received in an effort to obtain the needed information.

Importance of Documentation

In any abatement case, documentation is critical. As I tell my clients, "The more paper, the better." Some examples of helpful documentation that may apply in your case are:

- Doctor's notes.

- Hospital admission/discharge records.

- Medical bills/statements.

- Bank statements/income statements/W-2 forms.

- Proof of financial hardship such as bankruptcy documents, unemployment benefits, foreclosure notices, or similar.

- Insurance claims.

- Photographs.

- Government agency statements, such as FEMA statements regarding a natural disaster.

- Newspaper (or internet-based) reports.

- Death certificates.

- Court documents related to divorce, custody, or other significant legal battles.

- Eviction notices.

- Termination notices.

- Copies of relevant correspondence to the IRS or others.

- Evidence that you have corrected the issue that caused the penalty.

- Documentation showing subsequent compliance with tax obligations.

- A detailed letter explaining the factors that caused the penalty and your efforts to comply, including names, dates, etc.

Remember that each case is unique, and the strength of your argument will depend on your unique circumstances. Of course, in addition to abatement for reasonable cause, your penalty may be abated if it resulted from an IRS error, a regulation or statute that provides for abatement, or an administrative waiver, such as the First Time Abate, discussed below.

If you file a request for abatement and the IRS denies it, you will receive a "Letter 854C" explaining the denial. You will have the opportunity to appeal if you think the IRS decision is in error. To do so, carefully follow the directions in your denial letter. Failure to meet the requirements will result in a denial of your appeal. When submitting your appeal, thoroughly explain why you believe the IRS should abate the penalty and include any relevant supporting documents.

You may be able to skip this process if you qualify for the "First Time Abate" program.

First Time Abate

The First Time Abate ("FTA") program is an excellent tool if you have only one year with a balance due. This relief program offered by the IRS will waive specific penalties if you have a clean compliance history with the IRS.[17] To qualify for First Time Abate, you must meet the following requirements:

1. You must not have had penalties for the three years prior to the year that incurred the penalty you are trying to abate.

2. You must have filed all currently required returns or extensions.

3. You must have paid or arranged to pay any taxes due. If you have an Installment Agreement in place, that will not disqualify you so long as your payments are current.

If you meet these requirements, you may request relief from the following penalties:

- Failure to File penalty under IRC 6651(a)(1) for tax returns, IRC 6698(a)(1) for partnership returns, or IRC 6699(a)(1) for S Corporation returns.

- Failure to Pay penalty under IRC 6651(a)(2) and/or IRC 6651(a)(3), payment not made on time.

- Failure to Deposit penalty under IRC 6656.

If you know the IRS will assess penalties on a return you are filing, you can submit the FTA request with your tax return. <u>The easiest way to request a First-Time Abate is to call the IRS and apply over the phone</u>. Depending on the penalty amount, the representative may review your account and verify your eligibility on the phone. If you are eligible, they will input the information to abate the penalty while you are on the call. In some cases, a written request must be made. It is an easy task to submit a written request for a First Time Abate. You may use *Form 843, Claim for Refund and Request for Abatement.* If you use *Form 843*, include a statement in section 7 that you are requesting First Time Abate. It should look like this:

I (we) request abatement of the above-referenced penalty pursuant to the First Time Abate administrative relief. I (we) have filed all required returns; I (we) have not had any unreversed penalties for three years prior to the period at issue; all taxes due have been paid [or are included in a current Installment Agreement.]

You may also send a letter containing the same information to the IRS at the address on the notice you received. Attach a copy of the notice to your *Form 843* or letter.

It is important to note that the FTA program only applies to penalties, not the underlying taxes owed. If you cannot pay your taxes, you may need to explore other relief options, such as an Installment Agreement or an Offer in Compromise.

Appeal of First Time Abate Denial

If the IRS denies your First Time Abate request, you can appeal if all of the following have occurred:

1. You received a letter that the IRS has assessed a penalty.

2. You sent a written request to the IRS asking them to remove the penalty.

3. The IRS denied your request.

4. You received a letter denying your request, which gives you your appeal rights.

You generally have 30 days from the rejection letter date to file your appeal. The rejection letter from the IRS will contain a specific deadline for an appeal.

IRS Forms and Publications Related to This Chapter:

- *Form 4506-T – Request for Tax Return Transcript*

- *Form 4506 – Request for Copy of Tax Return*

- *Form 843 – Claim for Refund and Request for Abatement*

CHAPTER 7:

Installment Agreements

An IRS payment plan, officially called an "Installment Agreement," provides you with a practical solution to address your tax debts if you cannot pay the full amount when due.[18] The IRS offers several different types of Installment Agreements that allow you to pay your bill over time, providing immediate relief from enforced collection. The Installment Agreement is the most common resolution to a past-due tax account balance. In 2023, the IRS established 2,696,963 new Installment Agreements with taxpayers. A total of 4,038,081 Installment Agreements were in effect at the end of fiscal year 2023.[19] This chapter explores the various Installment Agreement options, eligibility criteria, application process, and the implications of entering into one of these agreements.

How to Enter Into an Installment Agreement

If you have an outstanding balance, you can enter into an Installment Agreement using one of three methods (as indicated below, some Installment Agreements require that you call):

1. Call the IRS at 800-829-1040. Based on your balance, the representative will assist you in setting up an Installment Agreement.

2. Complete and mail a *Form 9465, Installment Agreement Request* to the address listed in the *Form 9465* instructions.

3. If you qualify, you can apply online at **IRS.gov/payments/online-payment-agreement-application**. You qualify to apply online if:

- For an Installment Agreement, you owe $50,000 or less in tax, penalties, and interest and have filed all required returns;

- For a short-term payment plan (paying in 180 days or less), you owe less than $100,000 in tax penalties and interest.

- While it is more convenient to apply online - and less intimidating, I have found that a person-to-person conversation on the phone may result in a better payment plan for you.

Installment Agreement – How to Pay

The IRS makes it easy to pay. When you enter an Installment Agreement online or by speaking with an IRS representative, you can choose your preferred payment method. Unless otherwise indicated by the specific payment plan, Installment Agreement payment options include:

- IRS Direct Pay. You can pay from your checking or savings account using the online IRS Direct Pay program. **IRS.gov/payments/direct-pay**.

- Automatic monthly payments from your bank account using the direct debit Installment Agreement.

- Pay electronically using the Electronic Federal Tax Payment System (EFTPS). This requires enrollment at **www.eftps.gov**.

- Pay using a credit/debit card or digital wallet (through a third party processor who will charge a fee). See **IRS.gov/payments/pay-your-taxes-by-debit-or-credit-card**.

- Mail your monthly payment by check, money order or cashier's check.

- Cash, up to $1,000 per payment at participating retail establishments. (**www.IRS.gov/payments/pay-with-cash-at-a-retail-partner**)

- In some cases, the IRS will allow a Payroll Deduction Installment Agreement.

Installment Agreement User Fees

The IRS charges setup fees to offset the cost of collections. However, the IRS adds the fees to your account balance so you do not have to come up with the extra money to enter into the agreement. For Installment Agreements, the setup fees are as follows:

- Direct Debit Installment Agreement setup fees are $31 if the application is completed online. If the application is made in person, by mail, or by phone, the fee increases to $107. If you meet the definition of a low-income taxpayer, the setup fee is waived (see *Form 13844, Application for Reduced User Fee for Installment Agreements* to determine if you qualify as a low-income taxpayer).

- Non-Direct Debit Installment Agreements cost $130 if the application is completed online. Otherwise, the cost is $225. If low income, the setup fee is $43.

- In order to reinstate a defaulted Installment Agreement, the fee is $89. This is reduced to $43 if low-income qualifications are met.

Penalty Reduction for Installment Agreements

The failure to pay penalty is generally assessed at ½ of one percent of your delinquent tax balance monthly. [20] To encourage timely tax return filing and to encourage you to enter into an Installment Agreement, this penalty is reduced to ¼ of one percent for any month in which an Installment Agreement is in effect. [21] This applies under the following conditions:

- The balances due are from an individual.

- The tax return was filed on time (including within the time allowed when a proper extension was filed).

- Far along in the collections process, the IRS will issue what is known as a Final Notice of Intent to Levy (via Notice LT11 or Letter 1058). When that is issued to the taxpayer, the failure to pay penalty is increased from ½ of one percent to 1 percent a month. If any of these notices have been issued, this penalty reduction will not be available. This is to encourage you to enter into Installment Agreements earlier in the collection process rather than waiting until the last minute.

Protection from Levy

As a general rule, the IRS will not issue a levy:

- While an Installment Agreement is pending (after you have submitted your request in writing or to an IRS representative on the telephone).

- For 30 days following the rejection of an Installment Agreement request.

- During a timely appeal of an Installment Agreement request.

- While an Installment Agreement is in effect.

- For 30 days following the termination of an Installment Agreement.[22]

Pros and Cons of Installment Agreements

There are several advantages to entering into an Installment Agreement with the IRS, including:

- The ability to pay off the tax debt over time and provide financial flexibility.

- Protection from more aggressive collections actions, such as wage garnishment or asset seizure.

However, there are also some potential disadvantages to consider, such as:

- The accrual of interest and penalties continues on the unpaid balance.

- There is a potential for default and further collection actions if payments are not made on time.

- The requirement to continue making payments over a longer period may impact your future cash flow.

- The IRS may file a Notice of Federal Tax Lien if the balance exceeds a certain threshold.

Types of Installment Agreements

Several types of Installment Agreements are available, depending on how much you owe, the period involved, and how long the IRS has to collect before they are barred by the CSED (Collection Statute Expiration Date). Most delinquent taxpayers can fit into one of these types of Installment Agreements, which offer relatively generous payment terms. The new Taxpayer Relief Initiative provides very generous payment terms without providing financial information, even if your balance is large. Details can be found in the Non-Streamlined Installment Agreement (NSIA) section below.

In the worst-case scenario, the IRS will request a monthly payment equal to the difference between your gross monthly income and your necessary living expenses.

Gross Income – necessary living expenses = monthly Installment Agreement payment

For purposes of an Installment Agreement, gross income includes income from all sources, including wages, dividends, interest, etc., even if the income is not taxable income. There are three types of allowable expenses:[23]

1. Allowable Living Expenses

These are based on standard amounts set forth by the IRS based on your location, household size, and other factors. They are explained further in the section below dealing with completing *Form 433-F, Collection Information Statement.*

2. Other Necessary Expenses

These expenses must meet the necessary expense test, defined as expenses required to provide for your and your family's health, welfare, and/or income production.

3. Other Conditional Expenses

These expenses may not meet the necessary expense test but may be allowable based on the circumstances of an individual case. For instance, they may be allowed if you qualify for the Six-Year Rule described below.

The type of Installment Agreement you are offered will depend on your specific circumstances. If you call the IRS to request an Installment Agreement, the representative will, after confirming your identity and reviewing your balances, ask you how much you were thinking of paying each month. Your answer should be, "*What is the smallest payment I can make to qualify for the Installment Agreement.*" Sometimes, the representative may push back with a statement about how making the largest payment possible will pay your balance quicker and reduce the penalties and interest you will pay. The best response to this statement would be, "*I'd like to keep the mandatory payment smaller to reduce the possibility of a default if I have some unexpected expenses. I will make additional payments against my liability as my finances allow.*" If the representative insists on a number from you, give a number at the low end of your desired payment amount range. They will plug the number into the computer. If it does not qualify, given the specifics of your account, they will give you the minimum amount necessary to enter into the Installment Agreement. You can always make larger or extra payments, but you will have to jump through some hoops to reduce or skip any payments.

Here is an overview of the types of Installment Agreements available:

- <u>Short-Term Payment Plan</u>: For balances up to $100,000 that will be paid fully within six months.

- <u>Guaranteed Installment Agreement</u>: If you owe less than $10,000 in tax debt and meet specific other requirements, you may qualify for a Guaranteed Installment Agreement, which does not require a full financial review.

- <u>Streamlined Installment Agreement</u>: If you owe between $10,000 and $50,000 in tax debt and meet certain other requirements, you may qualify for a Streamlined Installment Agreement. Streamlined Installment Agreements do not require a full financial review.

- <u>Non-streamlined Installment Agreement (NSIA)</u>: If you owe more than $50,000 in tax debt or do not meet the requirements for other Installment Agreements, you may qualify for a Non-Streamlined Installment Agreement. In some cases, this type of agreement does not require a financial review and in others a full financial review may be necessary.

- <u>Partial Payment Installment Agreement</u>: If you cannot pay your total tax debt before the CSED, you may qualify for a Partial Payment Installment Agreement. This allows you to enter into an Installment Agreement even if it won't fully satisfy your tax liability.

The IRS representative should place you into the Installment Agreement that fits your circumstances. If you find that a particular Installment Agreement type works best for you, you can request it by name when you speak with the representative. A more detailed treatment of the different payment plans follows.

Short-Term Payment Plan

For repayment periods with a maximum duration of 180 days and balances up to $100,000, you can set up a short-term payment plan by calling the IRS at 800-829-1040 or applying online using the IRS's online payment agreement tool at **IRS.gov/OPA**. Do not use *Form 9465 Installment Agreement Request* if you are applying for a Short-Term Payment Plan. There are <u>no setup fees</u> to set up a short-term payment plan. If you are self-employed or an independent contractor, you can apply for this plan as an individual (rather than as a business).

Guaranteed Installment Agreement

To qualify for a Guaranteed Installment Agreement:[24]

- The tax due (excluding penalties and interest) must not exceed $10,000;

- You (and spouse, if joint return) during the past five years have not:

    ○ Failed to file any required return;

    ○ Failed to pay tax;

    ○ Entered into an Installment Agreement.

- The maximum payment period is three years.

The best way to apply for a Guaranteed Installment Agreement is to call the IRS at 800-829-1040 or apply online using the IRS's online payment agreement tool at **IRS.gov/OPA**.

Streamlined Installment Agreement

A Streamlined Installment Agreement allows you to pay past-due taxes over an extended timeframe without providing income, expense, and asset information to the IRS. To request this payment arrangement, you can use the Online Payment Arrangement application online (**IRS.gov/OPA**), complete and submit *Form 9465 Installment Agreement Request*, or call 800-829-1040.

Who Qualifies for a Streamlined Installment Agreement?

- Those who have filed all of their required income tax returns.

- Individuals (and sole proprietors who are no longer in business) with a total balance (including tax, interest, and penalties) of up to $50,000.

- Business taxpayers with balances of up to $25,000 (tax only, not including penalties or interest).

Benefits of Streamlined Installment Agreements

- Repayment period of six years. The repayment period may be less if the entire liability cannot be paid by the CSED (Collection Statute Expiration Date).

- There is no need to complete and submit a *Form 433-F Collection Information Statement*. This document, required for certain Installment Agreements, contains detailed information about your income, expenses, and assets. Not having to complete *Form 433-F, Collection Information Statement* will save you a substantial amount of time.

- A Notice of Federal Tax Lien is not required to be filed on balances up to $25,000.
- If the payments are made via a direct debit from your bank account or a payroll deduction on balances up to $50,000, a Notice of Federal Tax Lien may not be filed.
- If you qualify for a Streamlined Installment Agreement, it is available even if you can afford to pay the liability in full.[25]

Direct Debit Streamlined Installment Agreements:

- These incorporate a monthly direct debit from your bank account or an automatic payroll deduction.
- These occur automatically, and you do not need to mail a check or sign in to your account to make the monthly payment.

Non-Streamlined Installment Agreements (NSIA)

If you owe more than $50,000 in tax debt or do not meet the requirements for other Installment Agreements, you may qualify for a Non-Streamlined Installment Agreement (NSIA).[26] In some cases a full financial review will be required. However, during the COVID-19 pandemic, the IRS instituted the Taxpayer Relief Initiative which included, among other things, easing of the requirements for an NSIA, and created a new category called "NSIA – Without Financial Review." The attributes of NSIA – Without Financial Review are as follows:

- To qualify, you must be an individual or an individual sole proprietor who is no longer in business.
- Your liability must not exceed $250,000.
- The payment plan must fully pay your liability before the Collection Statute Expiration Date (CSED). This date is generally 10 years from the date the tax was assessed.
- You must not be asking for a levy to be released.
- Managerial approval is required.
- A Notice of Federal Tax Lien may be recorded to protect the government's interest.
- You must apply by phone. 800-829-1040.

If you do not qualify for the NSIA – Without Financial Review, you may still qualify for an NSIA. In this case, the following will apply:

- The agreement must pay the liability in full within six years or the CSED, whichever is sooner.

- A completed *Form 433-F Collection Information Statement* is required for a financial review by the IRS.

- Expenses deemed reasonable do not need to be substantiated.

- All expenses may be allowed if:

  - You can establish that you can stay current with the payment of subsequent tax years, including estimated tax payments.

  - The tax liability, including projected penalties and interest, can be fully paid within six years and within the CSED.

  - Expense amounts are deemed to be reasonable.

- The "One Year Rule" states that if you cannot fully pay within six years, you may be given up to one year to modify or eliminate excessive expenses. This would include, for example, an expensive car payment or expensive housing costs which may fall outside the allowable expense limits.

- You must apply by phone. 800-829-1040.

Partial Payment Installment Agreement (PPIA)

If the amount of money you can pay the IRS in a monthly Installment Agreement will not fully pay your account before the CSED (Collection Statute Expiration Date), you may still be able to enter into an Installment Agreement under the following conditions: [27]

- You must complete and submit a *Form 433-F Collection Information Statement.*

- You may be required to provide supporting financial information, e.g., pay stubs, bank statements, lease or mortgage payment statements, etc.

- Equity in assets may be examined by the IRS and, if appropriate, used to satisfy or partially satisfy the tax debt, although utilization of equity is not always a condition of a Partial Payment Installment Agreement[28]

- The IRS may require you to make a good faith attempt to borrow against or sell assets.[29]

- The IRS may file a Notice of Federal Tax Lien.

- Management review and approval is required.

- By definition, the PPIA will not pay off the entire debt before the expiration of the CSED. Generally, the PPIA will not extend the CSED, although, under certain circumstances, the IRS will require a limited CSED waiver.[30] A CSED waiver extends the time the IRS has to collect your debt.

- The agreement is subject to periodic review. A change of financial circumstances may result in a modified payment amount (including the possibility of a larger payment).

How the PPIA Payment is Calculated

The IRS will review your financial statement to determine the amount you can afford to pay. This amount is your gross income from all sources minus the necessary living expenses as described above.

Payroll Deduction Installment Agreement (PDIA)

In some cases, a Direct Debit Installment Agreement is not practical. For those who are wage earners, a Payroll Deduction Installment Agreement may be appropriate. To enter into this type of agreement, I highly suggest you contact the IRS by phone first. These agreements require the use of *Form 2159, Payroll Deduction Agreement*. This form has sections for you and your employer to complete and is only available in cases where the employer will agree to the terms. For example, the United States Postal Service does not accept these agreements. These agreements are relatively rare and only used when one of the previously listed types of agreements would not work, for instance, if you do not have a conventional bank account from which a direct debit can be made. [31]

Completing the Form 433-F Collection Information Statement

In some cases, the IRS will require you to complete a *Form 433-F Collection Information Statement*. This form and its instructions can be found online at **www.irs.gov/pub/irs-pdf/f433f.pdf**. This financial statement serves two functions for the IRS. First, it identifies assets (viewed by the IRS as "levy sources" or assets they may be able to seize in the worst-case scenario). Second, it helps the IRS determine your income and necessary living expenses. It does not matter how much money you owe the IRS; they will accept payments based on your ability to pay. In an Installment Agreement, the IRS will not demand payment in excess of the difference between your gross income and your necessary living expenses. The *Collection Information Statement* helps determine what that number is. The main parts of the *Collection Information Statement* are as follows:

Personal Identification Information

The first section of the Collection Information Statement asks for your name, address, telephone, social security number and the same information about your spouse as well as the number of dependents you have. It also asks about your business, if you have one, its employer identification number and number of employees.

Assets/Liabilities

The second part of the Collection Information Statement asks you to list your assets and their values. This includes bank accounts, investment accounts, virtual currency, real estate and the "catch all" category of "Other Assets." Some assets are easy to value, such as your bank account or investment account. Other assets, such as your house and cars are more difficult to value. The internet can provide you with estimates that you can use. You can use sites such as Zillow.com or Realtor.com to estimate the value of your home. Local brokers will usually give you an estimate of your home's value as well. Kelly Blue Book is a good online source for vehicle values (kbb.com). Don't be overly optimistic when estimating the values. Consider the potential selling price of the asset if you had to sell it quickly and without making cosmetic improvements that you might typically undertake to enhance its marketability. If you receive an estimate from a third party or online, be sure to keep a copy to substantiate your claim of value.

Income and Expenses

In Section F, provide your employment information as indicated. In Section G, list your non-wage income. There are eight fields that identify different types of income and a ninth field, "other," in case you have other income that does not fit into one of the listed categories.

Section H addresses "Monthly Necessary Living Expenses." This section will be the focus of the IRS when determining how much income you have after expenses that they deem necessary. There are certain expense limits imposed by the IRS. These limits are contained in the Collection Financial Standards and I will explain these standards before we discuss the specific entries in Section H. In the current inflationary environment, it is possible one or more of your expense categories exceeds the limits set by the IRS collection standards. If possible, gather any documentation that substantiates the expense so it is more likely the IRS will accept your figures rather than the lower collection standard figures.

Collection Financial Standards and Section H of the Collection Information Statement

When I was a new tax lawyer, the IRS made subjective judgments on what was considered a necessary living expense. With the implementation of collection financial standards, the rules are much more objective, although there is some wiggle room based on your unique circumstances. Some expenses that fall within the standard amounts are allowed without question or proof. If your expenses exceed these standards, you may have to substantiate (prove) the expenses and defend the expense as being necessary under your circumstances. Some of the standards apply nationwide (National Standards), while others depend upon the region of the country in which you reside (Local Standards). The current amounts can be accessed at **www.IRS.gov/businesses/small-businesses-self-employed/collection-financial-standards**

National Standards

The IRS uses the same National Standards nationwide when examining taxpayers' financial statements. The IRS will allow, as necessary living expenses, the national standard amount for your family size without questioning the amount actually spent.[32] These National Standards apply to the following expenses:

National Standards: Food, Clothing and Other Items

- Apparel and services, including shoes, clothing, laundry/dry cleaning, and clothing/shoe repair.
- Food. This includes all your meals at home and away from home.

- Housekeeping supplies, including laundry, and cleaning supplies; other household products, such as cleaning and toilet tissue, paper towels, and napkins; lawn and garden supplies, postage and stationery; and other miscellaneous household supplies.

- Personal care products and services. This includes hair care products, barber and beautician services, oral hygiene products, shaving needs, cosmetics, perfume, bath preparations, deodorants and similar products.

- Miscellaneous. Some examples include credit card payments, work expenses, bank fees and charges, reading material, school books and supplies for elementary through high school age dependents, etc. This category can also be used for any portion of expenses that exceed the allowable living expense standards.

National Standards: Out-of-Pocket Health Care Expenses

- Medical services.
- Prescription drugs.
- Medical supplies, such as eyeglasses and contact lenses.

These expenses are allowed in addition to amounts paid for health insurance, or individual shared responsibility payments, if applicable. Taxpayer verification of the out-of-pocket expenses is not required unless the amount claimed exceeds the National Standard. If your out-of-pocket expenses exceed the standard, the IRS will allow the expense if proper documentation is provided.

Local Standards

The IRS recognizes that the cost of living differs considerably across various regions of the United States. To address these differences, the Local Standards were established, offering allowable expense guidelines that reflect the cost of living in different locations. There are two sets of local standards, one for housing and utilities and the other for transportation costs.

Local Standards: Housing and Utilities

The current amounts and locations to determine the applicable Local Standards for housing and utilities are found at **www.IRS.gov/businesses/small-businesses-self-employed/collection-financial-standards**

The criteria for housing and utilities are as follows:[33]

1. Housing expenses include mortgage payments, rent, property taxes, maintenance and repair, insurance, homeowner association and condo fees.

2. Utilities include gas, electricity, water, heating oil, bottled gas, trash collection, wood and other fuels, septic cleaning, cable TV, internet, telephone and cell phone.

Additional notes regarding Local Standards for housing and utilities:

- These expenses are usually considered necessary only for the primary residence. Other housing expenses will be allowed only if disallowance would cause economic hardship based on your unique facts and circumstances. If your case includes an additional property, be prepared to demonstrate how disallowance of these expenses would create an economic hardship.

- The number of people allowed for determining family size will equal the total number in your household including you and your dependents. The IRS will by default use the number you used on your tax return. If your circumstances have changed, they will allow a deviation from last year's dependent number.

- Unlike the National Standards which are allowed without question, the Local Standards provide that you will only be allowed the lower of the amount claimed and verified or the Local Standard amount. My experience is that the IRS will generally accept your figures if they do not exceed the Local Standard amount. It is not uncommon for the IRS to allow more if you can provide documentation to demonstrate that the expenses are necessary. With the recent red-hot inflation, it is more common for taxpayers to exceed these Local Standard amounts.

Local Standards: Transportation

Transportation costs consist of two parts: **ownership costs** (for monthly loan or lease payments) and **operating costs** (maintenance, repairs, insurance, fuel, registration, licenses, inspections, parking and tolls).

The ownership costs provide a maximum allowance for the lease or purchase of up to two automobiles (if you are single, you are generally allowed one vehicle). This amount is standardized across the country. However, allowable operating costs are broken down by the metropolitan area of your residence. Current transportation standards can be accessed here: **www.IRS.gov/businesses/small-businesses-self-employed/local-standards-transportation**

You may be able to negotiate a larger allowance by providing objective evidence of your costs. These might include:

- Copies of invoices for registration, insurance, maintenance, tolls, and parking.
- Fuel receipts or calculations based on your necessary travel.
- Costs of travel for employment, healthcare, and other necessary functions will carry more weight if you can provide details such as distance of required travel and average fuel costs in your area, which you can obtain using a search engine or website such as GasBuddy.com.

There is a single, nationwide amount allowed for public transportation. As with the other standards, if your expenses exceed the current allowance, provide documentation substantiating the cost of the transportation and provide information showing that such transportation is necessary and you should be able to negotiate the allowance of the higher amount.

Section H.1. of Form 433-F

This section addresses:

- Food
- Housekeeping Supplies
- Clothing and Clothing Services
- Personal Care Products and Services
- Miscellaneous

For this section, the **National Standards for food, clothing, and other items** apply nationwide. You are allowed the total National Standards amount monthly for your family size without questioning the actual amount spent. For instance, as of January 2024, the total amount allowed without question for this category of expenses would be $841 for one person and $1,389 for a family of two. As the number of family members increases, the allowable amount increases.

The National Standard amount should be entered in the "Total" box in Section H.1. If your expenses exceed the National Standard amount, each box should be filled in, and you should be prepared to substantiate the costs and demonstrate the necessity of the excess cost.

Section H.2. of Form 433-F

This section addresses

- Gas/Insurance/Licenses/Parking/Maintenance, etc.
- Public Transportation

For this section, the **Local Standards for Transportation** are used. There are two parts to the Transportation standards. First, is the **ownership cost**, consisting of monthly loan or lease payments. This amount is entered in Section C, "Other Assets." The ownership cost is the same nationwide. As of January 2024, the allowed ownership cost is $629 for one car and $1,258 for two cars. The second part of the standards addresses **operating costs,** which cover gas, insurance, licenses, parking, maintenance, etc. This varies by region. For example, in January 2024, allowable operating costs for one car in Minneapolis are $214, while one car in Los Angeles would be allowed $339 in monthly operating costs. My experience with the transportation standards is that they are frequently exceeded by the actual costs. Historically, the IRS has been reasonable in allowing the excess amount if the expenses are supported by supplemental details, including items such as local tolls, local gas costs, individual insurance rates, etc. Be prepared to provide details if your expenses exceed the standards.

A nationwide allowance for Public Transportation is allowed at the rate of $218/month as of January 2024.

If the amount claimed for any of the transportation costs is more than the standards, you must provide documentation to substantiate those expenses as necessary living expenses.

Section H.3. of Form 433-F

This section deals with:

- Rent (mortgages are entered in Section B)
- Electric, Oil/Gas, Water, Trash
- Telephone, Cell, Cable, Internet
- Real Estate Taxes and Insurance (to the extent they are not included in your mortgage payment)
- Maintenance and Repairs

The **Local Standards: Housing and Utilities** are designated by the county of residence. For instance, in January of 2024, a family of one in Miami would be allowed $2,212 in monthly housing and utility expenses. This increases to $2,598 for a family of two.

You are allowed the standard amount or the actual amount, whichever is less. If the amount claimed is more than the total allowed by the standard, you must provide documentation to substantiate those expenses as necessary living expenses. With today's high housing costs, this is an area where you may need to substantiate higher expenditures. Copies of lease/mortgage documents, as well as utility bills, may be helpful if your expenses exceed the standards.

Section H.4. of Form 433-F

Section H.4. addresses medical expenditures. Health insurance costs are allowed and are not limited by a national or local standard. Out-of-pocket costs are addressed by the National Standards: Out-of-Pocket Health Care Expenses.[34] As of January 2024, the standard for those under 65 is $79 per month. For those 65 and older, the amount is $154. For those of us who are not in our early years, this amount is easily exceeded. Consider gathering your medical expenditure receipts so you can substantiate higher monthly expenses if that is the case.

Section H.5. of Form 433-F

This section deals with "other" expenses. They are listed as follows:

- Child/Dependent Care

- Estimated Tax Payments (Federal and State)
- Term Life Insurance
- Retirement (employer required)
- Retirement (voluntary)
- Union Dues
- Delinquent State and Local Taxes (minimum monthly payment)
- Student Loans (minimum monthly payment)
- Court Ordered Child Support
- Court Ordered Alimony
- Other Court-Ordered Payments
- Other

Take some time to ensure you have included all of your expense items. Some of these items will necessarily involve a reasonable estimate, but the more items you can substantiate with invoices or receipts, the stronger your case will be.

Sole Proprietors and Form 433-F

If you are self-employed, you can still use *Form 433-F*. The first section of the form will ask for your business name, EIN, type of business and number of employees other than the owner. Be sure to include business information where indicated elsewhere in the form. You will enter your business accounts in Section A and other business assets in Section C. In Section E1, you will enter accounts receivable and Section E2 you will enter the requested information if your business accepts credit cards payments (e.g. Visa) and/or virtual currency wallet, exchange or digital currency exchange. Your net monthly business income will be entered in Section G. While not requested on the form, the representative you speak with may request an income (profit/loss) statement.

Form **433-F** (February 2019)	Department of the Treasury - Internal Revenue Service **Collection Information Statement**

Name(s) and Address	Your Social Security Number or Individual Taxpayer Identification Number
	Your Spouse's Social Security Number or Individual Taxpayer Identification Number

☐ If address provided above is different than last return filed, please check here	Your telephone numbers Home: Work: Cell:	Spouse's telephone numbers Home: Work: Cell:
County of Residence		

Enter the number of people in the household who can be claimed on this year's tax return including you and your spouse. Under 65 _____ 65 and Over _____

If you or your spouse are self employed or have self employment income, provide the following information:

Name of Business	Business EIN	Type of Business	Number of Employees *(not counting owner)*

A. ACCOUNTS / LINES OF CREDIT

PERSONAL BANK ACCOUNTS Include checking, online, mobile (e.g., PayPal), savings accounts, money market accounts. (Use additional sheets if necessary.)

Name and Address of Institution	Account Number	Type of Account	Current Balance/Value	Check if Business Account
				☐
				☐

INVESTMENTS Include Certificates of Deposit, Trusts, Individual Retirement Accounts (IRAs), Keogh Plans, Simplified Employee Pensions, 401(k) Plans, Profit Sharing Plans, Mutual Funds, Stocks, Bonds, Commodities (Silver, Gold, etc.), and other investments. If applicable, include business accounts. *(Use additional sheets if necessary.)*

Name and Address of Institution	Account Number	Type of Account	Current Balance/Value	Check if Business Account
				☐
				☐

VIRTUAL CURRENCY (CRYPTOCURRENCY) List all virtual currency you own or in which you have a financial interest (e.g., Bitcoin, Ethereum, Litecoin, Ripple, etc.). *(Use additional sheets if necessary.)*

Type of Virtual Currency	Name of Virtual Currency Wallet, Exchange or Digital Currency Exchange (DCE)	Email Address Used to Set-up With the Virtual Currency Exchange or DCE	Location(s) of Virtual Currency *(Mobile Wallet, Online, and/or External Hardware storage)*	Virtual Currency Amount and Value in US dollars as of today *(e.g., 10 Bitcoins $64,600 USD)*

B. REAL ESTATE Include home, vacation property, timeshares, vacant land and other real estate. *(Use additional sheets if necessary.)*

Description/Location/County	Monthly Payment(s)	Financing		Current Value	Balance Owed	Equity
☐ Primary Residence ☐ Other		Year Purchased	Purchase Price			
		Year Refinanced	Refinance Amount			
☐ Primary Residence ☐ Other		Year Purchased	Purchase Price			
		Year Refinanced	Refinance Amount			

C. OTHER ASSETS Include cars, boats, recreational vehicles, whole life policies, etc. Include make, model and year of vehicles and name of Life Insurance company in Description. If applicable, include business assets such as tools, equipment, inventory, etc. *(Use additional sheets if necessary.)*

Description	Monthly Payment	Year Purchased	Final Payment *(mo/yr)*	Current Value	Balance Owed	Equity
			/			
			/			

D. CREDIT CARDS *(Visa, MasterCard, American Express, Department Stores, etc.)*

Type	Credit Limit	Balance Owed	Minimum Monthly Payment

TURN PAGE TO CONTINUE

Catalog Number 62053J	www.irs.gov	Form **433-F** (Rev. 2-2019)

E. BUSINESS INFORMATION Complete E1 for Accounts Receivable owed to you or your business. *(Use additional sheets if necessary.)* Complete E2 if you or your business accepts credit card payments. Include virtual currency wallet, exchange or digital currency exchange.

E1. Accounts Receivable owed to you or your business

Name	Address	Amount Owed
	List total amount owed from additional sheets	
	Total amount of accounts receivable available to pay to IRS now	

E2. Name of individual or business on account

Credit Card *(Visa, Master Card, etc.)*	Issuing Bank Name and Address	Merchant Account Number

F. EMPLOYMENT INFORMATION If you have more than one employer, include the information on another sheet of paper. *(If attaching a copy of current pay stub, you do not need to complete this section.)*

Your current Employer *(name and address)*	Spouse's current Employer *(name and address)*

How often are you paid *(check one)*
☐ Weekly ☐ Biweekly ☐ Semi-monthly ☐ Monthly
Gross per pay period
Taxes per pay period *(Fed)* *(State)* *(Local)*
How long at current employer

How often are you paid *(check one)*
☐ Weekly ☐ Biweekly ☐ Semi-monthly ☐ Monthly
Gross per pay period
Taxes per pay period *(Fed)* *(State)* *(Local)*
How long at current employer

G. NON-WAGE HOUSEHOLD INCOME List monthly amounts. For Self-Employment and Rental Income, list the monthly amount received after expenses or taxes and attach a copy of your current year profit and loss statement.

Alimony Income		Net Rental Income		Interest/Dividends Income	
Child Support Income		Unemployment Income		Social Security Income	
Net Self Employment Income		Pension Income		Other:	

H. MONTHLY NECESSARY LIVING EXPENSES List monthly amounts. (For expenses paid other than monthly, see instructions.)

National Standards

1. Food / Personal Care See instructions. If you do not spend more than the standard allowable amount for your family size, fill in the Total amount only.

	Actual Monthly Expenses	IRS Allowed
Food		
Housekeeping Supplies		
Clothing and Clothing Services		
Personal Care Products & Services		
Miscellaneous		
Total		

2. Transportation

	Actual Monthly Expenses	IRS Allowed
Gas / Insurance / Licenses / Parking / Maintenance etc.		
Public Transportation		
Total		

3. Housing & Utilities

	Actual Monthly Expenses	IRS Allowed
Rent		
Electric, Oil/Gas, Water/Trash		
Telephone/Cell/Cable/Internet		
Real Estate Taxes and Insurance *(if not included in B above)*		
Maintenance and Repairs		
Total		

4. Medical

	Actual Monthly Expenses	IRS Allowed
Health Insurance		
Out of Pocket Health Care Expenses		
Total		

5. Other

	Actual Monthly Expenses	IRS Allowed
Child / Dependent Care		
Estimated Tax Payments		
Term Life Insurance		
Retirement *(Employer Required)*		
Retirement *(Voluntary)*		
Union Dues		
Delinquent State & Local Taxes *(minimum payment)*		
Student Loans *(minimum payment)*		
Court Ordered Child Support		
Court Ordered Alimony		
Other Court Ordered Payments		
Other *(specify)*		
Other *(specify)*		
Other *(specify)*		
Total		

Under penalty of perjury, I declare to the best of my knowledge and belief this statement of assets, liabilities and other information is true, correct and complete.

Your signature	Spouse's signature	Date

Catalog Number 62053J   www.irs.gov   Form **433-F** (Rev. 2-2019)

All Installment Agreements; Important Terms

<u>To negotiate any Installment Agreement you must be in compliance with filing, withholding, and estimated tax payment requirements.</u>[35] Your Installment Agreement contains terms that you should review so you can avoid having your Installment Agreement terminated (called a "default" by the IRS). Here is a brief overview of some of the more important terms:

- You must file all federal tax returns on time.
- You must pay any taxes on new liabilities on time.
- You must pay all payments under the Installment Agreement on time.
- The agreement is based on your current financial status. If the IRS has information that this has changed, they may want to modify it. The IRS may request updated financial information, and you are required to provide it. If they ask for updated financial information and you do not provide it, they may terminate your existing agreement.
- If the IRS terminates your agreement, they will have all the tools at their disposal to collect the remaining amount due, including seizing your assets.
- If you default on your agreement and the IRS terminates the agreement, the IRS will consider reinstating it at your request, in which case you will be liable for a reinstatement fee of $89 (or $43 if you meet the then-current income threshold). This fee will be added to your balance, so it is unnecessary to pay it upfront.
- A Notice of Federal Tax Lien may be filed by the IRS.
- The IRS may terminate the agreement if they find that collection of taxes is in jeopardy, for example, if they find out you are fleeing to another country to try to escape your tax liability.

Changes to Existing Installment Agreements & Emergency "Skip"

Financial circumstances can change. If you have an Installment Agreement in place with the IRS and you can no longer afford it, call the IRS at 800-829-1040 and explain your circumstances. If you need a short reprieve, ask to skip a month. Those requests are generally granted if you are current on your payments, and the IRS will generally allow two "skips" in a 12-month period without defaulting your Installment

Agreement.[36] If you have a direct debit Installment Agreement, call at least ten days before your scheduled payment so the IRS can suspend the payment in time. You can also ask if you can reduce the monthly payment amount and stay within your Installment Agreement category. If so, they can adjust your payment downward without having to take new financial information from you.

Depending on the balance and payment terms, they may ask for updated financial information. Financial information is provided to the IRS using *Form 433-F Collection Information Statement.* Save time by penciling in the numbers before you call. The IRS will usually take this information over the phone to adjust your payment plan.

Installment Agreement Effect on Collection Statute Expiration Date (CSED)

The Collection Statute Expiration Date is the last day the IRS is legally allowed to collect your taxes. It is generally ten years from the date of assessment. Installment Agreements generally[37] do not extend the Collection Statute Expiration Date ("CSED") during the time the agreement is in effect. However, there will be an extension of the CSED for the following periods:

- While the Installment Agreement is pending (during analysis and prior to implementation).
- For 30 days following rejection or termination of an Installment Agreement.
- If the rejection or termination is appealed, then for the period of time that Appeals is considering the appeal of the rejection or termination.

How to Appeal the Denial of an Installment Agreement

You have the right to appeal if your request for an Installment Agreement is denied. If you received a notice granting you a right to a Collection Due Process appeal, you may file such an appeal on *Form 12153, Request for a Collection Due Process or Equivalent Hearing* if you are within the timeframe. If you have missed the deadline, you may file for an equivalent hearing, or you may apply for an appeal under the Collection Appeals Program using *Form 9423, Collection Appeal Request.* The Appeals Officer will take a fresh look at your case. You should emphasize (and support with any available documentation) how the payment of anything in excess of the amount you have offered will result in economic hardship.

Special Rules for Payroll Tax

Payroll taxes are different from income taxes. They are a special tax levied on wages and salaries paid to employees to fund FICA (Social Security and Medicare) as well as unemployment taxes. A portion is paid through payroll deductions, and the rest is paid directly by the employer. The IRS is stricter with employers who owe payroll tax.

In-Business Trust Fund Express Installment Agreement

If you have a business with employees, you can qualify for an In-Business Trust Fund Express Installment Agreement[38] by calling the IRS Business and Specialty Tax assistance line at 800-829-4933 or online through your online IRS account. If you qualify for this program, you will not be required to submit financial statements. The requirements are as follows:

- You owe $25,000 or less at the time you establish your Installment Agreement. You may pay down your debt prior to entering into the agreement to qualify.

- If you owe over $10,000, you must agree to a direct debit agreement in which the IRS debits your account monthly for the payments.

- You must be current with all filing and payment requirements.

- The maximum term for repayment is 24 months. If the CSED (Collection Statute Expiration Date) expires earlier than 24 months, you agreement will have to fully pay the liability before the CSED.

Other Payroll Tax Installment Agreements

If your business cannot pay operating expenses and current taxes, the IRS policy is to go straight to enforced collection, such as levy and seizure.[39] Otherwise, they reason, you will just continue to accrue additional liabilities, something the IRS calls "pyramiding." They would prefer to shut your business down rather than allow additional liabilities.

If you can pay operating expenses and current taxes, the IRS will explore options for an Installment Agreement. However, your finances will be highly scrutinized. Expect to provide *Form 433-B, Collection Information Statement for Businesses,* along with supporting documentation, including bank statements and other proof of expense. The IRS will search for any equity you have in real property and personal property (such as cars). They will likely request that you sell assets or borrow on equity to make payments on your delinquent taxes.[40] If your business is a separate legal entity, such as a corporation, they may attempt to hold you personally liable under the Trust Fund Recovery Penalty.[41]

IRS Forms and Publications Related to This Chapter:

- *Form 9465 – Installment Agreement Request*

- *Form 433-D – Installment Agreement*

- *Form 433-F – Collection Information Statement*

- *Form 433-A – Collection Information Statement for Wage Earners and Self-Employed Individuals*

- *Form 433-B - Collection Information Statement for Businesses*

- *Publication 1660 – Collection Appeal Rights*

- *Form 9423 – Collection Appeal Request*

- *Form 12153 – Request for Collection Due Process or Equivalent Hearing*

CHAPTER 8:

Currently Not Collectible Status ("CNC")

Currently Not Collectible ("CNC") status is a temporary status granted by the IRS if you cannot make payments toward your past due tax debt without causing economic hardship. If you are placed in this status, the IRS will stop its collection activities, but interest and penalties will continue to accrue on your account. The IRS says they will review this status annually by requesting an updated *Form 433-F, Collection Information Statement.* My experience is that they often take longer to follow up. If the IRS requests updated financial information, be sure to promptly comply. If you do not, they will resort to enforced collection such as levy and seizure.

Application Process

There is no IRS form to request CNC status. The quickest way to apply is by telephone. You will need to give the representative your financial information, so I recommend completing a *Form 433-F Collection Information Statement* ahead of time. Doing so will allow you to refer to the form to answer the questions posed by the representative.

To complete the process, phone the IRS (800-829-1040) and tell the representative that you are experiencing financial hardship and would like to be placed in a Currently Not Collectible status. The representative will ask a host of questions and may ask questions related to the *Form 433-F, Collection Information Statement,* including your income, tax withholdings, necessary living expenses, etc. In some cases, the IRS will ask that you submit the *Form 433-F, Collection Information Statement.* I have had some cases where the IRS has asked to review three months' of bank statements or asked for proof of unemployment when the taxpayer was unemployed. In such a case, a copy of an unemployment check stub or correspondence from the unemployment office should do the trick. Based on your specific information, the representative can recommend a CNC status, but the file will be forwarded to management for final approval. These requests are typically approved by management within a couple of weeks. If approved, you will receive a letter detailing the terms of the CNC status.

Benefits and Drawbacks of CNC Status

The main benefit of CNC status is that the IRS will stop its enforced collection activities, such as levies and garnishments. This can provide much needed relief if you are experiencing financial hardship. However, interest and penalties will continue to accrue on the tax debt. The IRS may periodically review your financial situation to determine if you are still eligible for CNC status. If your financial situation improves, they may no longer be eligible for CNC status, and the IRS may resume its collection activities. If so, they will not undertake enforced collection without giving you the opportunity to explore other resolution options such as an Installment Agreement or Offer in Compromise.

TIP: When I call the IRS for a client who is eligible for CNC status, I usually say that the client wants to enter into an Installment Agreement, but a review of the finances shows that there is no excess money left at the end of the month. I will then review the information with the IRS on the phone, and if the financial information calls for it, the IRS will place the taxpayer in a CNC status. If they don't suggest a CNC status, I will.

How to Appeal the Denial of CNC Status

There is no appeal available for the denial of the Currently Not Collectible status itself, but you may use either the Collections Due Process Appeal or the Collections Appeals Program, as the case may be, for the underlying enforcement action the IRS is proposing (e.g., Notice of Intent to Levy or Notice of Federal Tax Lien)

IRS Forms and Publications Related to This Chapter:

- *Form 433-F – Collection Information Statement*

- *Publication 1660 – Collection Appeal Rights*

- *Form 9423 – Collection Appeal Request*

- *Form 12153 – Request for Collection Due Process or Equivalent Hearing*

CHAPTER 9:

Offer in Compromise ("OIC")

I f you find yourself unable to pay your tax debt in full, the Offer in Compromise program may offer you a lifeline. [42] An OIC allows you to settle your tax liability for less than the full amount owed, providing a path to financial relief. Congress authorized this type of relief in Section 7122 of the Internal Revenue Code. This section grants the IRS the discretion to accept less than full payment based on your ability to pay, doubt as to the accuracy of the assessment or exceptional circumstances that would make full payment unjust. The criteria for an OIC are stringent. In 2023, taxpayers submitted 30,163 offers and 12,711 were accepted. [43]

Match Your Scenario to the Proper Offer in Compromise

There are a number of types and subtypes of Offers in Compromise. These examples can help you determine which type may work for you:

OIC Based on Doubt as to Liability (DATL)

You owe $25,000 in tax. You have a bona fide doubt as to the liability for the underlying tax even though it was legally assessed. For example, the IRS proposed an increase in tax and you did not dispute it in time, resulting in an additional assessment. You can file an OIC DATL.

OIC Based on Doubt as to Collectibility (DATC)

You owe $25,000 in tax. Your Reasonable Collection Potential is $10,000. The IRS can settle for the payment of the Reasonable Collection Potential ($10,000). The Reasonable Collection Potential is what the IRS determines you can pay given your income and asset values. This will be addressed in detail below.

OIC Based on Doubt as to Collectibility with Special Circumstances (DATCSC)

You owe $25,000 in tax. Your Reasonable Collection Potential is $10,000. However, requiring you to pay the $10,000 will create a hardship, or payment of the $10,000 would be deemed unfair or against public policy due to unique or unusual circumstances. In this case, the matter can be settled for a fair amount under the circumstances.

OIC Based on Effective Tax Administration (ETA)

You owe $25,000 in tax. Your Reasonable Collection Potential is $40,000. Under your circumstances, payment of the $25,000 in tax would create a hardship or, due to unique or unusual circumstances, it would be deemed unfair or against public policy. In this case, the amount can be settled for an amount that would be fair under the circumstances.

There are three main categories of Offers in Compromise:

Based on Doubt as to Collectibility ("DATC")

This is the most common type of Offer in Compromise. This is used when the liability is more than you can pay prior to the expiration of the CSED (Collection Statute Expiration Date). When applying for this type of OIC, you will submit financial statements that demonstrate your income, expenses, assets and liabilities. If you cannot fully pay your liability before the CSED, the IRS will consider your income, expenses, assets and liabilities to determine the "Reasonable Collection Potential" which is the minimum the IRS will take in settlement of your case. The factors and calculations are explained fully below.

Based on Doubt as to Liability ("DATL")

This type of OIC is used to settle an assessment in which there is a bona fide doubt as to whether the assessment is correct. This type of OIC would be used in the event the IRS assessed taxes against you, perhaps after an audit, and the tax law was misapplied or the assessment was otherwise in error. If the time to contest the audit via the administrative remedies (e.g. appeals) has passed, you have the choice of suing the IRS federal court (assuming the statute of limitations has not passed) or you can file an OIC based on Doubt as to Liability. Under these circumstances, an OIC will probably be the most cost effective option.

Effective Tax Administration ("ETA")

This type of offer is used when you are not eligible for either of the above types of offers, but enforcement of the liability would cause economic hardship (failure of the ability to meet basic living expenses) or if the acceptance of the Offer in Compromise would support effective tax administration based upon public policy or equity grounds.

Each will be addressed in detail below.

Offer Based on Doubt as to Collectibility ("DATC")

An Offer in Compromise based on Doubt as to Collectibility (commonly called "DATC") is a program authorized by Congress and implemented by the IRS that allows the IRS to accept a settlement for less than the full amount of tax, penalties, and interest owed. The goal of the IRS in these cases is to collect as much money as possible at the earliest possible time and at the least cost to the government.[44] In some cases, the IRS determines acceptance of the OIC is not in the best interest of the government. In that case, the IRS may reject it, even if it passes the mathematical qualifications explained herein.[45]

Important note: As with most negotiations with the IRS, you must be current on filing your tax returns and must be current on estimated tax payments or tax withholding from your wages in order to submit an OIC. You can review your *Form W-4* with your employer to ensure your withholding figures are correct.

Benefits and Drawbacks of Offers in Compromise

An OIC's primary benefit is that it allows you to settle your tax debts for less than the full amount owed. This can relieve financial stress and provide a fresh start. However, the OIC process can be lengthy and complex, and there is a high rejection rate. Additionally, if your OIC is accepted, you must comply with all tax obligations for the next five years or risk having your OIC revoked. If your OIC is revoked, you will owe all of the money that was compromised, including tax, interest, and penalties.

Public Review of Limited Offer Information

For one year following acceptance of an Offer in Compromise, members of the public can request to view limited information regarding a specific OIC by submitting a completed Offer in Compromise Public Inspection File Form. This form requires the party requesting the information to identify the specific Offer in Compromise for which the information is requested.

Application Process

The OIC application process involves filing a *Form 656, Offer in Compromise*, along with a *Form 433-A (OIC), Collection Information Statement for Wage Earners and Self-Employed Individuals* as well as a *Form 433-B (OIC), Collection Information Statement for Businesses* if your business is a corporation, partnership or LLC. Supporting documentation and the application fee (unless waived) must also be submitted. The IRS may request additional information during the review process, and it is important to respond promptly to any such requests.

You will submit your financial information on *Form 433-A (OIC)*. This form is very similar to *Form 433-F* used for Installment Agreements. See "Completing the *Form 433-F Collection Information Statement*" in the Installment Agreement chapter for detailed guidelines for completing this form as well as the application of the Collection Financial Standards used by the IRS when reviewing your finances.

If the offer does not meet the threshold for being a processable offer (e.g. not signed, you are not in compliance, required payment not submitted) the IRS will return the offer to you. If the OIC meets the threshold requirements, the IRS will send you a letter that acknowledges receipt of the offer. This letter will also indicate a date by which the examiner will follow up with you. When the offer examiner contacts you, the examiner will typically ask for verification of some of the figures claimed on the *Form 433-A (OIC)* which was submitted with the offer. After performing their analysis, the examiner will reject the offer, propose acceptance of the offer, or propose an increased amount that will be deemed acceptable. This process usually takes about a year, with simple wage earner cases sometimes taking less time and more complex or self-employed cases taking a bit longer. IRS has a "prequalifier" website you can use to enter your information and your offer amount. The website will tell you if you qualify based on the information submitted. The website address is: **IRS.treasury.gov/oic_pre_qualifier/**

IRS Two-Step Analysis

The IRS performs a two-step analysis to determine if the Offer in Compromise based on Doubt as to Collectibility is acceptable.

First, The IRS will review your assets (specifically, the equity you have in your assets) as well as what you can afford to pay in monthly payments after payment of your monthly necessary living expenses. If the IRS determines the tax can be paid in full before the CSED if you were to liquidate your assets and enter into an Installment Agreement, the IRS will not consider the offer. This is based on the determination that you can fully pay the liabilities.

Second, if the IRS determines that the account cannot be fully paid, they will determine whether the offer exceeds the **Reasonable Collection Potential**.[46] The Reasonable Collection Potential is the sum of the quick sale value of your assets plus future income determined by the "Lump Sum" or "Periodic Payment" calculation as described below.

Payment Options for your OIC

There are two different types of payment options available to pay the Offer in Compromise settlement.

Lump Sum Method

The first is the "**Lump Sum**" method. This method contemplates a lump sum payment or the lump sum divided into six equal payments. The first payment, which consists of 20% of the offer amount, is made with the submission of the offer application. The remaining balance is paid in five or fewer payments within five or fewer months of the acceptance date. If you meet the low-income certification guidelines, the first payment is not required to be submitted with the application. Instead, you can pay it within 30 days of acceptance.

Calculation of Offer Amount with Lump Sum Payment

A lump sum payment is an offer that is paid in five or fewer payments in five months or less. In this case, the minimum offer is the sum of these two figures:

1. Future Income, as defined by the IRS.[47] This is specified as your projected gross monthly income, less allowable expenses. This monthly net income is multiplied by 12 for a lump sum payment Offer in Compromise.[48]

2. The Net Realizable Equity in your assets.[49] The Net Realizable Equity is defined as the "Quick Sale Value" minus the amount owed to secured lienholders senior to an IRS lien, minus any exemption amounts that apply to that asset class. Quick Sale Value is defined as the estimate of the price a seller could receive in circumstances where financial pressures motivate the owner to sell in a short period, usually 90 days or less.

Advantages of the Lump Sum Payment Method:

- The amount of the OIC will be lower than the Periodic Payment method because, with the Lump Sum method, the calculation of future income takes into account 12 months of future income rather than the 24 months that is used with the Periodic Payment method.

- Aside from the initial 20% payment, no payments are required during the evaluation of the OIC. Payments only begin after acceptance.

Disadvantages of the Lump Sum Payment Method:

- The total amount of the offer must be paid within five months of acceptance, resulting in a shorter payment period than the Periodic Payment method.

Periodic Payment Method

The second payment option is the Periodic Payment method. In this case, you split the payments into equal monthly payments to be made over 6-24 months. Unlike the Lump Sum method, you are required to submit the first payment with the offer application and continue making the payments while the offer is being considered. Generally speaking, if the OIC is rejected, the payments are not returned to you, rather they are applied to your account. If you meet the low-income certification guidelines, no payment is required until the offer is accepted.

Calculation of Offer Amount with Periodic Payment Method

Periodic payments are offers in which the offered amount is paid over a period of six to 24 months. In this case, the minimum offer is the sum of these two figures:

1. Future Income, as defined by the IRS.[50] This is specified as your projected gross monthly income, less allowable expenses. This monthly net income is multiplied by 24 for an Offer in Compromise paid over a period of 6 to 24 months.[51]

2. The Net Realizable Equity in your assets.[52] The Net Realizable Equity is defined as the "Quick Sale Value" minus the amount owed to secured lienholders senior to an IRS lien, minus any exemption amounts that apply to that asset class. Quick Sale Value is defined as the estimate of the price a seller could receive for the asset in circumstances where financial pressures motivate the owner to sell in a short time, usually 90 days or less.

Advantages of the Periodic Payment Method

- The payments are spread over a longer period, assisting in affordability.

Disadvantages of the Periodic Payment Method

- Monthly payments are required during the evaluation of the OIC.
- If the OIC is rejected, the IRS will keep the payments that have been made.
- The offer will be higher than the Lump Sum method because, with the Periodic Payment method, the calculation of future income takes into account 24 months of future income rather than the 12-month period that is used in the Lump Sum method.

Low Income Fee Waiver & Payment Deferral

If you meet the low-income certification found on page two of *Form 656, Offer in Compromise*, no application fee is charged, and under either the Lump Sum method or Periodic Payment method, no funds are required to be submitted with the OIC. All payments are deferred until the acceptance of the OIC.

Calculating Future Income on Form 433-A (OIC)

The following necessary living expenses are subtracted from your gross monthly income (including income amounts that are not taxable):

1. Tax withholding from your paycheck or estimated taxes if you are making estimated tax payments.

2. Food, clothing, housekeeping, personal care products, and small miscellaneous personal expenses, including minimum credit card payments. A reasonable estimate may be used.

3. Mortgage or rental payments for your home.

4. Property taxes, insurance, HOA fees, maintenance, utilities, cable TV, internet, and telephone service (including cell service).

5. Real and personal property tax.

6. Public transportation costs. A reasonable estimate may be used.

7. Vehicle loan or lease payments.

8. Vehicle operation costs (gas, registration, insurance, maintenance). A reasonable estimate may be used.

9. Health insurance premiums

10. Out-of-pocket healthcare costs. The average monthly cost of drugs, supplies, services, etc.

11. Court-ordered payments (e.g., alimony, child support).

12. Child/dependent care payments.

13. Life insurance premiums for term insurance.

14. Secured debts.

15. Mandatory retirement contributions.

If you own a sole proprietor business, the business income is reduced by the business expenses. The resulting net monthly business income becomes part of your gross monthly income for purposes of the above calculations. If you own an interest in a partnership, the same analysis would apply to your percentage interest in the partnership income and expense.

The amounts allowed by the IRS are not unlimited. The IRS has imposed a maximum allowable expense for many of these items. For instance, at the time of this writing, the allowable monthly amount for food, housekeeping, clothing, personal care products, and miscellaneous expenses ranges from $841 for one person to $1,993 for four persons in the household. These maximums are intended as guidelines. If the examiner determines the maximum allowable amount is inadequate to provide for the applicant's basic living expenses, a deviation will be allowed.[53] In such a case, you will need to substantiate the expenses and explain how they are necessary, given your unique circumstances. You can find the Collection Financial Standards published by the IRS on their website.[54] These figures are updated periodically, and the maximum allowed expenses can vary by your county of residence to take into account the difference in the cost of living in different parts of the country. See my detailed explanation of Collection Financial Standards in the Installment Agreement Chapter.

Calculating Net Realizable Equity on Form 433-A (OIC)

The "Net Realizable Equity" is defined as the "Quick Sale Value" minus the amount owed to secured lienholders senior to an IRS lien, less any exemption amounts that apply to that asset class.[55] The IRS acknowledges that if you were forced to liquidate your assets quickly, there may not be enough time to obtain full fair market value. Quick Sale Value is defined as the estimate of the price a seller could receive for the asset in circumstances where financial pressures motivate the owner to sell in a short time, usually 90 days or less. In some cases, like cash, the Quick Sale Value will equal the full fair market value. For non-cash assets, the rule of thumb is that the Quick Sale Value is 80% of the full fair market value. To arrive at this figure, simply multiply the full fair market value by 0.8. This is a rule of thumb only and current market conditions may justify deviation from this general rule.[56]

Here is a list of common assets and how this discount is applied to each:

Cash

Because cash is immediately available without discount, there is no discount to arrive at a Quick Sale Value. The IRS will allow a reduction in the cash balance by the allowable monthly living expenses. Additionally, there is a $1,000 exemption that applies to cash. Therefore, for purposes of the offer, cash balances are only considered to the extent they exceed $1,000 plus the monthly allowable living expenses.[57]

Securities

Publicly traded stocks and bonds have a Quick Sale Value of the fair market value less transaction costs and current years' taxes due to any capital gain.[58]

Life Insurance

The Quick Sale Value is the cash surrender value minus any loan balances.

Retirement Plans

The Quick Sale Value is the market value of the account minus transaction costs. The reduction in current market value should take into account tax consequences and withdrawal penalties.

Furniture, Fixtures, and Personal Effects

Typically, your declared value will be used.[59] Eighty percent of the market value is used as a Quick Sale Value.

Vehicles, Aircraft, and Water Vessels

Eighty percent of the fair market value is used as the Quick Sale Value. Appraisals may be necessary in some cases, but typically, a value can be found using a trade association guide (e.g., Kelly Blue Book for cars). The private party value is used, not the trade-in value.[60] Additionally, the amount of $3,450 is subtracted as an exemption for each car (two vehicles for joint taxpayers and one vehicle for single taxpayers).

Real Estate

The fair market value is provided by the OIC applicant and should be accompanied by an appraisal or broker price opinion (from a disinterested broker). This is reduced by 20% to arrive at a Quick Sale Value. Any loan balances secured by liens senior to the Notice of Federal Tax Lien are subtracted from the Quick Sale Value to arrive at the Net Realizable Equity.

Tools of the Trade

For individuals and sole proprietorships, the Fair Market Value is reduced by 20% to arrive at a Quick Sale Value. This is reduced by any secured loans that are senior to the Notice of Federal Tax Lien. Furthermore, there is an exemption amount for tools of the trade of $5,400 at the time of this writing.

There are many specific circumstances and examples provided in the Internal Revenue Manual in Section 5.8.5.5 and the sections that follow.

Documents to Submit with the Offer in Compromise

You are required to submit the following supporting documents with the Offer in Compromise:

1. *Form 433-A (OIC), Collection Information Statement for Wage Earners and Self Employed Individuals*

2. *Form 433-B (OIC), Collection Information Statement for Businesses.* This form must be submitted if you have an interest in a business that is not a sole proprietorship.

3. If you have a business, including a sole proprietorship, include a current profit and loss statement covering the most recent 6-12 month period.

4. Copies of the most recent pay stub or earnings statement from each source.

5. Copies of most recent investment and retirement account statements.

6. Copies of most recent statements for all other sources of income.

7. Copies of the most recent three months' of bank statements for personal accounts.

8. Copies of the most recent six months' of bank statements for business accounts.

9. Copies of the most recent loan statements (e.g., mortgage, vehicle loans).

10. List of notes or accounts receivable.

11. Verification of delinquent state or local tax accounts, including monthly payments, if applicable.

12. Copies of court orders related to any child or spousal support reported on your *Form 433-A (OIC)*.

13. Copies of trust documents, if applicable.

14. Documentation to support any special circumstances described in the "Explanation of Circumstances" on *Form 656, Offer in Compromise.*

15. Though not required, I have my clients submit a letter with their Offer in Compromise outlining the following:

    a. The circumstances that led to the liability.

    b. Good faith efforts made by the client to address the liability.

c.   The circumstances that prevent the full payment of the liability, including the hardships a requirement for full payment would entail.

d.   Reiteration of special circumstances, such as a medical condition or disability, old age, or other relevant factors that apply to the case.

e.   An assurance that future liabilities will be properly paid.

Requirement to Update Financial Statements

In some cases, the processing time for an Offer in Compromise can take over a year. When the delay is long enough that the initial application financial information may be outdated, the IRS may request updated financial information. The Internal Revenue Manual provides that it may be appropriate to request updated information from you if over 12 months have passed since the submission of the application and it appears significant financial changes have occurred. This decision is left to the judgment of the examiner and his or her supervisors.[61]

Factors that Affect Acceptance or Rejection

The IRS considers several factors when evaluating an OIC, including income, expenses, assets, and ability to pay. The IRS may also consider whether you have made good-faith efforts to pay the tax debt, and whether accepting the OIC would promote effective tax administration.

Application Fee

The application fee is $205 and must be submitted with the offer unless you meet the low-income certification guidelines. The Low-Income Certification only applies to individuals and sole proprietors. On page two of *Form 656 Offer in Compromise*, there is a table to assist in determining if you meet the low-income threshold. There are two ways to qualify:

1.   If the adjusted income on your most recently filed personal income tax return (*Form 1040*) is less than the corresponding amount on the Low-Income Certification table, given your family size and location.

2. Your household's gross monthly income from *Form 433-A (OIC)* (the financial statement that is part of the Offer in Compromise Form) multiplied by 12 is less than the corresponding amount on the Low-Income Certification table, given your family size and location.

If you qualify under either method, do not send money with the offer.

How to Appeal the Rejection of an OIC

As an additional safeguard, if an examiner has decided to reject an offer, the case must first undergo an independent administrative review to ensure such rejection is proper under the circumstances.[62] If the rejection is upheld by the independent administrative review, you can appeal to the IRS Independent Office of Appeals.[63] They will take a fresh look at the case.

Form 13711, Request for Appeal of Offer in Compromise, is specifically tailored to appeal a rejection of an Offer in Compromise. The IRS should send copies of their Income/Expense and Asset/Equity Tables along with the rejection letter. Those tables show the values and calculations used by the IRS. These values are likely the source of disagreement. When submitting your appeal, identify specific findings you disagree with and supply documentation supporting your case if possible. Be sure to submit your appeal within the 30-day appeal period.

Important Post-Acceptance Terms

After your offer is accepted and you've completed the payments, it might seem like everything is settled. However, there is a crucial point to keep in mind. The terms of the Offer in Compromise stipulate that the IRS retains the right to restart collection action if you don't adhere to the tax laws, fail to file your tax returns promptly, or neglect to pay your taxes on time during the five years following the acceptance of your offer. This five-year period ends at the end of the year following the fifth anniversary of the acceptance of your Offer in Compromise.

Doubt as to Collectibility with Special Circumstances ("DATCSC")

An Offer in Compromise Based on Doubt as to Collectibility with Special Circumstances can be considered by the IRS when:

1. You cannot fully pay the tax due, and

2. The Reasonable Collection Potential is less than the amount owed (if it is more than the amount owed, an OIC-ETA is the appropriate relief), and

3. You have proven special circumstances (based on hardship or public policy/equity) that warrant acceptance for less than the amount of the calculated Reasonable Collection Potential.[64]

Normally in a Doubt as to Collectibility case, you must offer at least the amount of the Reasonable Collection Potential. However, under certain circumstances, the IRS can consider hardship, public policy, and equity to conclude that an amount less than the Reasonable Collection Potential is an acceptable settlement amount. The analysis performed by the IRS will be the same as when they examine an Offer in Compromise - Effective Tax Administration (ETA) case.

The factors establishing special circumstances under DATCSC are the same as those considered under ETA.[65]

DATCSC Based on Hardship

The first type of special circumstance is where the Reasonable Collection Potential - the amount the IRS estimates they can collect from you - is less than your total liability, but special circumstances exist that would create an economic hardship if the amount of the Reasonable Collection Potential was paid. In this situation, an acceptable offer amount is determined by examining your financial information and the hardship that would result if certain assets, or a portion of them, were used to pay the full amount of the Reasonable Collection Potential. An example is as follows:

The taxpayer has a $125,000 liability and a Reasonable Collection Potential of $100,000 (resulting in a collection potential less than the liability). The IRS determines that the taxpayer will need $75,000 of the reasonable collection potential to meet his or her living expenses, including substantial medical expenses *over the foreseeable future. The remaining $50,000 should be considered the acceptable offer amount in this case.*

Note: If the Reasonable Collection Potential exceeds the liability, the taxpayer is not eligible for an Offer in Compromise based on Doubt as to Collectibility but may qualify for an Offer in Compromise based on Effective Tax Administration (ETA).

DATCSC Based on Public Policy/Equity

The second type of special circumstance is where there are compelling public policy or equity considerations that provide sufficient basis for compromise. Examples of an Offer in Compromise Doubt as to Collectibility based on Public Policy/Equity are as follows:

1. An IRS processing error directly caused your liability and would otherwise have been avoided. If other administrative remedies (e.g., abatements, etc.) do not put you back in the same position that you would have occupied if the error had not been made, a compromise would be appropriate.[66]

2. Erroneous advice from the IRS caused you to incur a tax liability that would not otherwise have been incurred. In these cases, you must be able to show through some form of documentation when the advice was provided and the IRS employee involved. If there is no other mechanism to adjust your account to reflect the amount that would have been owed had the IRS not made an error, accepting an Offer in Compromise is appropriate.[67]

3. If the IRS's actions or inaction unreasonably delayed the resolution of your case and interest or penalty abatement is not available, compromise may still be warranted if the circumstances are sufficiently compelling.[68]

4. Relief may be available if you can demonstrate that a third party's criminal or fraudulent act is directly responsible for the tax liability.[69] Proper documentation and evidence should be included, as well as evidence that you have taken reasonable precautions to prevent criminal or fraudulent acts.

5. Compromise may be appropriate where there is clear and convincing evidence that rejecting the Offer in Compromise and pursuing other collection alternatives would negatively impact the community in which you live or do business. In other words, you provide essential services to the

community that would be lost if the tax liability was collected in full. Businesses that typically qualify under this provision are not-for-profit, charitable, or exempt organizations. A specific example is outlined in the Internal Revenue Manual as follows: *"A non-profit organization provides quality health and human services to indigent, low-income, and under-served residents in two counties. Rejecting the offer and pursuing collection action for full payment would force the organization to choose between paying the delinquent taxes and providing competent medical care."* [70]

6. Compromise may be appropriate if you are incapacitated and unable to comply with the tax laws. The IRS will consider accepting an offer that would approximate the amount you would have been assessed had you been able to comply promptly. [71]

7. There may be other circumstances involved in a case that would lead a reasonable third party to conclude that accepting an Offer in Compromise would be fair, equitable, and promote effective tax administration. Other factors not specifically referenced in the Internal Revenue Manual may be present to support the conclusion that the case presents compelling public policy or equity considerations sufficient to justify acceptance of the offer. [72]

Application Process for DATCSC

The application process for an Offer in Compromise based on Doubt as to Collectibility – Special Circumstances will be the same as the application process with a standard Doubt as to Collectibility (DATC) case, with one exception:

Because you are asking to pay less than the Reasonable Collection Potential, you must explain the special circumstances that would cause an undue hardship or be against public policy/equity if you were required to pay the full amount of the Reasonable Collection Potential.

To complete the application specific to the DATCSC, you will do the following:

1. Complete *Form 433-A (OIC), Collection Information Statement for Wage Earners and Self-Employed Individuals.* In Section 8 of the form, you will be asked to enter the figures from your assets and your income to arrive at an offer amount. Enter the amount as calculated. This is your Reasonable Collection Potential, and in a regular DATC case, this amount is the minimum offer you can make. However, with a DATCSC offer, this will not be the amount you offer.

2. Check the "Doubt as to Collectibility" box in Section 3 of *Form 656, Offer in Compromise*.

3. In Section 4 of *Form 656, Offer in Compromise*, <u>enter the amount you are able to pay</u> due to your special circumstances under the "Lump Sum" heading or the "Periodic Payment" heading, depending on which payment plan you will use.

4. Attach a separate sheet of paper to the *Form 656, Offer in Compromise*. At the top of this page, write your name, your social security number, and "Form 656." Title the page as follows: **Statement of Special Circumstances in Support of Offer in Compromise Based on Doubt as to Collectibility with Special Circumstances.**

5. On this separate attachment, explain in as much detail as possible, the factors that support your case for hardship or public policy/equity as explained earlier in this chapter. Attach supporting documents if any such documents are available. The more paper the better.

6. In addition to this statement of special circumstances, be sure to submit all supporting documents listed at the end of *Form 433-A (OIC), Collection Information Statement for Wage Earners and Self-Employed Individuals.*

Offer in Compromise Based on Doubt as to Liability ("DATL")

Once taxes have been assessed, they are difficult to reverse. The standard course to reverse an assessment is to pay the tax in full and then apply for a refund from the IRS.[73] If the refund is denied, you must then sue the government for a refund in the District Court or Claims Court. This is costly and requires you to pay the tax in full first. An administrative alternative to suing the government for a refund is applying for an Offer in Compromise based on Doubt as to Liability.

To be eligible to apply for an Offer in Compromise Based on Doubt as to Liability, you must have a legitimate dispute regarding your tax liability. This dispute could involve errors in the assessment, incorrect calculations, or a disagreement about whether you are responsible for the tax debt.

Application Process for DATL

The application is made on *Form 656-L, Offer in Compromise, Doubt as to Liability (DATL)*. Unlike the doubt as to collectibility offers, you do not need to submit a collection information statement (these are the forms that outline your finances).[74] There is no application fee for this type of OIC, so do not send a deposit or application fee with your OIC. You must, however, include a written statement explaining why the liability is incorrect and addressing the validity of the tax assessment (or a portion thereof).[75] The application should include the reasons underlying your doubt as to your liability and all supporting documentation to support your position. Section 5 of *Form 656-L, Offer in Compromise, Doubt as to Liability (DATL)*, is titled "Explanation of Circumstances." This is where you explain why you believe the tax is incorrect. There are only six lines available in this section, so you will need to attach additional sheets to ensure you provide a thorough explanation of why the IRS should compromise your liability. Use as much detail as possible and be sure to attach any documents that support your position.

Unlike doubt as to collectibility offers, offers based on doubt as to liability are reviewed by the Examination function of the IRS. These are the same people who would be involved in the examination (audit) of your tax returns. The reason for their assignment to these tasks is their familiarity with the laws and regulations as they apply to the determination of the proper amount of tax to be assessed.[76] Upon completion of the review by the IRS, they may negotiate a settlement or resolution based on their findings in order to reduce the tax liability or correct errors in the assessment.

If you and the IRS cannot come to an agreement, the matter may be appealed. The IRS is required to provide you with your appeal rights as well as information related to how to submit the appeal. *Form 13711, Request for Appeal of Offer in Compromise*, is specifically tailored for appeals of a rejection of an Offer in Compromise. When submitting this form, you will identify specific findings that you disagree with, and you should submit any supporting documentation for your case.

Offer in Compromise Based on Effective Tax Administration ("ETA")

Three elements must exist for the IRS to consider an Offer in Compromise Based on Effective Tax Administration ("ETA"):

1. A liability has been or will be assessed against you before acceptance of an OIC.
2. The sum of net equity in assets, future income, and the other components of collectibility making up the Reasonable Collection Potential must be greater than the amount owed (in other words, you can fully pay the liability).

Robert C. Platt, Esq., JD, LLM

3. Exceptional circumstances exist, such as the collection of tax would create an economic hardship, or there are compelling public policy or equity considerations that provide sufficient basis for compromise.[77]

The previous chapters focused on Offers in Compromise based on doubt as to collectibility and doubt as to liability. There is another, less frequently used Offer in Compromise based on what is called "Effective Tax Administration." Congress authorized the IRS to accept less than full payment in satisfaction of a tax liability and instructed the IRS to provide guidelines that allow consideration of hardship, public policy, and equity. This resulted in the category of offers in compromise called "Offer in Compromise based on Effective Tax Administration" (also referred to as "ETA.").

The Offer in Compromise based on Effective Tax Administration is only available if you do not qualify for an offer based on Doubt as to Collectibility or Doubt as to Liability.[78] There are two types of cases that will qualify to be compromised under the Offer in Compromise based on Effective Tax Administration.

ETA Based on Hardship

The first type of case is where the Reasonable Collection Potential (the amount the IRS figures they can collect from you) exceeds the liability, but special circumstances exist that would create a hardship if the debt were to be fully paid. In this case, an acceptable offer amount is determined by analyzing the financial information and the hardship that would be created if certain assets, or a portion of certain assets, were used to pay the liability.[79] An example used by the IRS is as follows:

The taxpayer has a $100,000 liability and a reasonable collection potential of $125,000 (resulting in a collection potential in excess of the liability). It is determined that the taxpayer will need $75,000 of the Reasonable Collection Potential to meet her living expenses, which include substantial medical expenses over the foreseeable future. In this case, the remaining $50,000 should be considered the acceptable offer amount.

Note: If the Reasonable Collection Potential is lower than the liability, and paying the Reasonable Collection Potential is either unjust or would create a hardship, an Offer in Compromise based on Doubt as to Collectibility with Special Circumstances (DATCSC) should be used.

ETA Based on Public Policy/Equity

The second type of Offer in Compromise based on Effective Tax Administration is an offer based on Public Policy/Equity. In this case, you would seek relief from the tax liability based on broader considerations beyond simple economic hardship. If, due to unusual circumstances, paying the full tax debt would be deemed unfair or against public policy, this type of Offer in Compromise would be appropriate.

Examples of ETA based on Public Policy/Equity

1. Your liability was directly caused by a processing error on the part of the IRS and would otherwise have been avoided. If other administrative remedies (e.g., abatements, etc.) do not put you back in the same position that you would have occupied if the error had not been made, a compromise based on Effective Tax Administration would be appropriate.[80]

2. Erroneous advice from the IRS caused you to incur a tax liability that would not otherwise have been incurred. In these cases, you must be able to show through some form of documentation when the advice was provided and the IRS employee involved. If there is no other mechanism to adjust your account so it reflects the amount that would have been owed had the IRS not made an error, acceptance of an Offer in Compromise based on Effective Tax Administration is appropriate.[81]

3. If actions or inaction of the IRS unreasonably delayed the resolution of your case and interest or penalty abatement is not available, compromise may still be warranted if the circumstances are sufficiently compelling.[82]

4. Relief under the Effective Tax Administration provisions may be available if you can demonstrate that the criminal or fraudulent act of a third party is directly responsible for the tax liability.[83] Proper documentation and evidence should be included, as well as evidence that you have taken reasonable precautions to prevent criminal or fraudulent acts.

5. Compromise under ETA may be appropriate where there is clear and convincing evidence that rejecting the Offer in Compromise based on Effective Tax Administration and pursuing other collection alternatives would have a significantly negative impact on the community in which you live or do business. In other words, if you provide essential services to the community that would be lost if the tax liability was collected in full. Businesses that typically qualify under this provision are

not-for-profit, charitable, or exempt organizations. A specific example is set forth in the Internal Revenue Manual as follows: *"A non-profit organization provides quality health and human services to indigent, low-income, and under-served residents in two counties. Rejecting the offer and pursuing collection action for full payment would result in forcing the center to choose between paying the delinquent taxes or providing competent medical care."*[84]

6. Compromise may be appropriate if you are incapacitated and unable to comply with the tax laws. The IRS will consider accepting an offer that would approximate the amount you would have been assessed had you been able to comply in a timely manner.[85]

7. There may be other circumstances involved in a case that would lead a reasonable third party to conclude that the acceptance of an Offer in Compromise based on Effective Tax Administration would be fair, equitable, and promote effective tax administration. Other factors not specifically referenced in the Internal Revenue Manual may be present to support the conclusion that the case presents compelling public policy or equity considerations sufficient to justify acceptance of the offer.[86]

Application Process for Offer in Compromise based on ETA (OIC-ETA)

As with the other types of offers, the Offer in Compromise based on Effective Tax Administration is submitted on *Form 656, Offer in Compromise.*

To complete the application specific to the OIC-ETA, you will do the following:

1. Complete *Form 433-A (OIC), Collection Information Statement for Wage Earners and Self-Employed Individuals.* In Section 8 of the form, you will be asked to enter the figures from your assets and your income to arrive at an offer amount. Enter the amount as calculated. This is your Reasonable Collection Potential, and in a regular DATC case, this amount is the minimum offer you can make. However, with an OIC-ETA offer, this will not be the amount you offer.

2. Section 3 of *Form 656* outlines the reason for the offer. There is a box for "Effective Tax Administration – Economic Hardship" and there is a box for "Effective Tax Administration – Public Policy or Equity." Check the appropriate box given the basis of your offer.

3. In Section 4 of *Form 656, Offer in Compromise*, <u>enter the amount you are able or willing to pay</u> due to your special circumstances under the "Lump Sum" heading or the "Periodic Payment" heading, depending on which payment plan you will use.

4. If your offer is based on economic hardship, attach a separate sheet of paper to *Form 656, Offer in Compromise.* At the top of this page, write your name, your social security number, and "Form 656." Title the page as follows: **Statement of Special Circumstances in Support of Offer in Compromise Based on Effective Tax Administration – Economic Hardship.** In this separate attachment, explain in as much detail as possible, the factors that support your case for hardship as explained earlier in this chapter. Attach supporting documents if any such documents are available.

5. If your offer is based on public policy or equity, attach a separate sheet of paper to the *Form 656, Offer in Compromise.* At the top of this page, write your name, your social security number, and "Form 656." Title the page as follows: **Statement of Special Circumstances in Support of Offer in Compromise Based on Effective Tax Administration – Public Policy or Equity.** In this separate attachment, explain in as much detail as possible why paying the full debt would be unfair, unjust, or inequitable and, as such, call into question the fairness of the tax system. Attach supporting documents if any such documents are available.

6. In addition to this statement of special circumstances, be sure to submit all supporting documents listed at the end of *Form 433-A (OIC), Collection Information Statement for Wage Earners and Self-Employed Individuals.*

Following an investigation by the IRS, including a review of the documents and evidence you submitted, the IRS may accept an offer based on what the IRS determines to be fair and equitable, given your exceptional circumstances. If you and the IRS cannot come to an agreement, or if the IRS rejects the offer, you will have the opportunity to appeal the decision. As with appeals of the other types of offers, the appeal is initiated by filing *Form 13711, Request for Appeal of Offer in Compromise* within the allowed appeal period, which is currently 30 days.

The IRS Prefers OIC DATC or DATL to ETA

The OIC based on ETA is an extraordinary remedy, meaning it is only granted in extreme and unusual cases, and is more difficult to approve than other types of offers. If an ETA offer is submitted, the IRS first determines if you qualify for an offer based on Doubt as to Collectibility or Doubt as to Liability.[87] Only if you fail to qualify for either of these will the IRS process the Offer based on Effective Tax Administration.[88]

Independent Administrative Review and Appeal

As an additional safeguard, if an examiner has decided to reject an OIC, the case must first undergo an independent administrative review to ensure such rejection is proper under the circumstances.[89] If the rejection is upheld by the independent administrative review, the case can be appealed to the IRS Independent Office of Appeals.[90] *Form 13711, Request for Appeal of Offer in Compromise* is specifically tailored for appeals of a rejection of an Offer in Compromise. When submitting this form, identify specific findings that you disagree with. You should submit any supporting documentation for your case. Be sure to appeal within the specified appeal period, currently 30 days.

IRS Forms and Publications Related to This Chapter:

- *Form 656 – Offer in Compromise*
- *Form 656-L Offer in Compromise (Doubt as to Liability)*
- *Form 433-A (OIC) – Collection Information Statement for Wage Earners and Self-Employed Individuals*
- *Form 433-B (OIC)- Collection Information Statement for Businesses*
- *Form 13711 – Request for Appeal of Offer in Compromise*

CHAPTER 10:

Bankruptcy

While bankruptcy is worthy of an entire book on the subject, it merits a quick overview when discussing the IRS collection procedure. Usually, other solutions to your tax problems will be more appropriate than bankruptcy, but there are cases where declaring bankruptcy can be a powerful tool in dealing with tax liabilities. The other administrative tax resolutions discussed in this book will work with most tax liabilities. Bankruptcy, on the other hand, limits the taxes that can be discharged (eliminated).

The two most common bankruptcy types for individuals are Chapter 7 and Chapter 13. A Chapter 7 bankruptcy is a type of personal bankruptcy that allows you to have most or all of your unsecured debts eliminated. Chapter 7 is means tested, meaning it is only available if your income does not exceed a certain threshold. Most Chapter 7 cases are known as "no asset" cases where you are able to keep all of your property due to statutory exemptions. If you have non-exempt property, a bankruptcy trustee can sell the non-exempt assets to pay or partially pay your creditors.

Tax liabilities other than income tax liabilities cannot be discharged. To discharge individual income tax liabilities, the following elements must be satisfied:

1. The tax liability must be from a tax return whose due date is over three years old. For example, a tax liability arising from 2023 income would be reported on a tax return on April 15, 2024. Such taxes would not be dischargeable in bankruptcy until after April 15, 2027 (if an extension was filed, the three years runs from the extended due date). Taking certain actions like requesting innocent spouse relief, applying for a taxpayer assistance order through the Taxpayer Advocate Service, or requesting a collection due process hearing may extend this three year period.

2. A late-filed tax return must be <u>filed more than two years before the bankruptcy</u> petition is filed. An IRS "Substitute for Return" is not considered a properly filed return for purposes of bankruptcy. If tax liability arises from a substitute for return, it will not be dischargeable (unless you file the proper return and meet the other elements).

3. The IRS must have <u>assessed the taxes at least 240 days before the bankruptcy</u> petition is filed. This element would apply to assessments resulting from an amended return or an audit.

4. The existence of an Offer in Compromise, US Tax Court case, or previous bankruptcy related to a particular tax year will extend the time periods identified above.

5. Taxes resulting from filing a fraudulent return or willfully attempting to evade or defeat such tax are not dischargeable.[91]

To complicate matters, a Notice of Federal Tax Lien filed before the bankruptcy still attaches to the equity in your property. Consultation with a bankruptcy lawyer is highly recommended.

Chapter 13 bankruptcy is a reorganization rather than a liquidation, and if you do not qualify for Chapter 7, Chapter 13 may provide relief. In a Chapter 13 case, if you have regular income, you can restructure and repay your debts over a three to five year period under the supervision of the court. In these cases, some of the debts may not be fully repaid. If a tax is discharged in bankruptcy, the penalties and interest related to that tax are also discharged. Tax debts that are not income tax, such as the payroll tax, or certain penalties, such as the Trust Fund Recovery Penalty (also dealing with payroll taxes), are not dischargeable.

Most collection clients have recent tax liabilities; therefore, bankruptcy is not ideal. However, if your tax liabilities are older and have been assessed for the requisite time, bankruptcy may be something to consider. Although you can file for bankruptcy on your own, the rules are so complex that I highly recommend professional assistance if you would like to explore bankruptcy.

PART III: SPECIAL CIRCUMSTANCES

CHAPTER 11:

Levy and Seizure

A levy is a legal seizure that dispossesses you of your property, such as money in your bank account, a house, or a car. A levy can also be against your rights in property, such as wages, income, bank accounts, retirement accounts, and Social Security payments. In non-tax cases, a court order is required before the seizure of someone's property. Not so with the IRS. However, there are rules they must follow, and they must afford you your due process rights (discussed below). Levies are a harsh collection technique and are not the first or preferred method of collection. I describe levies to my clients as "attention-getting" devices. It is relatively easy to ignore collection letters from the IRS. It is difficult to ignore the disappearance of the money in your bank account or getting a paycheck with a fraction of the money you earned during your pay period. In 2023, the IRS issued 286,270 levies on third parties (banks, investment accounts, wage garnishments).[92]

Three Requirements Before a Levy Can Take Place

1. Your tax is assessed, and the IRS has sent you a bill.

2. You neglect to pay the tax (or make alternate arrangements, such as an Installment Agreement);

3. The IRS sends you a Final Notice of Intent to Levy and Notice of your Right to a Hearing at least 30 days before the seizure.[93] Unless you are given this notice in person or the IRS leaves the notice at your home or place of business, the IRS must mail this notice to you via Certified Mail.[94] It is not necessary that you actually receive the notice. Merely mailing the notice to your last known address is sufficient. The IRS must then wait for the appeal period to lapse or wait until your appeal is concluded if you file your appeal on time.

The fact that the IRS can take most of your property and income is unsettling. However, you should note that this action is usually taken after repeated attempts by the IRS to bring you into compliance. Typically, a series of letters is sent, the last of which is a letter sent by certified mail. You have the right to appeal the proposed levy for 30 days following the issuance of the Notice of Intent to Levy. During that period, the IRS will not levy. After the passage of the appeal period, the IRS may levy one or more of your assets. In most cases, the IRS will levy assets held by third parties (such as a bank or your employer) because that is easier than seizing assets in your possession, such as a car.

Property Exempt from Levy

While the IRS has broad levy authority, there are some items that are exempt from levy:[95]

1. Clothing and school books.

2. Fuel, provisions, furniture, and personal effects with a maximum exemption of $6,250 in value.

3. Books and tools of trade, business, or profession with a maximum of $3,125 in value.

4. Unemployment benefits.

5. Undelivered mail.

6. Certain annuity and pension payments. These include payments under the Railroad Retirement Act, Railroad Unemployment Insurance Act, special payments to one who has been entered on the Army, Navy, Air Force, and Coast Guard Medal of Honor Roll, and the Survivor Benefit Plan (this provides beneficiaries with a portion of a military retiree's retirement pay in the event of the retiree's death).

7. Workers' Compensation payments.

8. That amount you are required by court order to pay for the support of your minor children.

9. There is a minimum exemption for wages, salary, and other income, to the extent it does not exceed the exempt amount. The exempt amount is equal to the standard deduction divided by 52 to arrive at a weekly exempt amount plus the "exemption amount."[96] The "exemption amount" refers to the amount allowed as a sort of deduction for the taxpayer and each member of his or her household that are dependents. (The "exemption amount is deemed to be zero for the years 2018 through 2025).[97]

10. Certain service-connected disability payments.

11. Certain Public Assistance Payments.

12. Assistance under the Job Training and Partnership Act.

13. In small deficiency cases (under $5,000), unless there are special circumstances, no levy shall be issued on your personal residence, real property or tangible personal property used in your trade or business.

What to Do if You Receive a Final Notice of Intent to Levy and Notice of Your Right to a Hearing

Time is of the essence, and you have certain rights that you should not let expire.

First, check the date on the letter. Don't be surprised if it is in the near future. The IRS postdates many of its letters to give you some extra time in the event of mail delays. In most cases, you will have 30 days to appeal using the Collection Due Process appeal. Make a note of when your appeal period ends.

Second: Call the IRS without delay. The phone number will be on your notice. Early mornings will subject you to the shortest hold times. Because it is unpleasant to call the IRS, you may be tempted to wait until the end of the 30-day period to call. Do not wait. If you let the time lapse, you will have fewer options or, eventually, you will have your assets seized.

Third: When speaking with the IRS representative, explore the different options to resolve your account. The IRS agent will ask about your finances. Depending on your circumstances, the IRS agent may place you in a temporarily non-collectible status or help you set up an Installment Agreement on the phone. You may also attempt to enter into an Installment Agreement online. My experience has been that you have more options and may get a better result by speaking with a representative live. You may be required to gather some financial information and call back later. When talking to the IRS agent about a possible Installment Agreement, they will ask how much you can pay monthly. Instead of offering an amount, ask what the smallest payment would be acceptable. Sometimes, they will offer you an amount that is acceptable to you without having to provide financial statements.

Fourth: This is important because due process is still on your side. If you have not been able to resolve the matter quickly and, at the latest, by the end of the Collection Due Process appeal period, complete and submit *Form 12153, Request for Collection Due Process or Equivalent Hearing,* [98] as instructed in your *Final*

Notice of Intent to Levy and Notice of Your Right to a Hearing. If you file the appeal on time, the IRS will not be able to levy until an appeals officer has heard your case. Your appeals hearing is informal and can be held via telephone, correspondence, or a face-to-face meeting. It is important to submit this form on time. It is much better to be early than late.

Fifth: It is advisable to file the appeal, even if you are still working with the IRS to resolve the case. If you are able to resolve your case while the appeal is pending, you can withdraw the appeal. Alternatively, the appeals officer, upon reviewing your case, will see that it has been resolved and notify you of the intent to cancel your appeal request.

Completing Form 12153, Request for Collection Due Process Hearing

The appeal form requests information regarding your identity, contact information, tax years at issue, and the basis of the appeal. In the case of a Final Notice of Intent to Levy, the basis will be "Notice of Proposed or Actual Levy."

Section 8 of the form will ask you to identify the reason for the hearing request. The most common reasons are "I am currently unable to pay due to financial hardship" and "I am unable to pay in full and would like a collection alternative." If either of these two boxes is checked, Section 9 allows you to choose a collection alternative, including "Installment Agreement," "Offer in Compromise," "Currently Unable to Pay," or "Other." In these cases, the IRS also requests that you submit financial statements (*Form 433-A* for individuals and *Form 433-B* for businesses). Submission is not required, but will expedite your case.

It is imperative to follow the instructions for the appeal and submit it to the proper address before it expires. I recommend certified mail so you have proof of timely mailing.

If you file your appeal late, you can request an "Equivalent Hearing." However, the Equivalent Hearing does not automatically suspend collections (i.e., the IRS can still levy), and you cannot petition the Tax Court for relief if your appeal is denied. If you file for an Equivalent Hearing, and while it is pending, I recommend you call the IRS and attempt to devise a collection alternative, such as an Installment Agreement. You can ask for, and the IRS will generally agree to hold any levies while you are actively working to resolve your case. In most cases, if you have applied for an Installment Agreement, Innocent Spouse Relief, or Offer in Compromise, the IRS will not levy while considering your requests. If, however, the IRS believes you are stalling or attempting to delay the collection action without a bona fide attempt at resolution, they may levy your assets.

Responding to Levies in General

Once the IRS gets its hands on the assets to pay your debts, it is difficult to get them to release the assets. However, the IRS will release a levy under the following circumstances:[99]

1. The liability is satisfied or is unenforceable due to the expiration of the Collection Statute Expiration Date (CSED).

2. Release of the levy will facilitate collection.

3. You have entered into an Installment Agreement.

4. The IRS determines that the levy is creating an economic hardship based on your financial condition.

5. The fair market value of the property exceeds such liability, and the release of the levy could be made without hindering the collection of the liability.

If you cannot afford to pay the tax in full, you can call the IRS and negotiate an Installment Agreement or, if your financial circumstances dictate, negotiate a Currency Not Collectible status and request the IRS levy be released based on financial hardship. A financial hardship exists if the loss of the funds will prevent you from meeting your basic living expenses.

It is always easier to negotiate with the IRS when your tax return filings are current. In many cases, the IRS will not negotiate until all your past-due returns are filed. However, it is important to note that once a hardship has been determined, a levy cannot be left in place to encourage the filing of unfiled returns.[100]

Levy on Wages, Salary, and Other Income (Sometimes Called "Garnishment")

A levy on your wages is one of the most unsettling IRS collection methods. This collection tool is used in the same manner as levying other assets, such as your bank account. The IRS does not expect to collect all of your taxes by way of levy, but they know if they hit your paycheck, you are likely to call and resolve your case. The levy against your wages will probably take most of your pay. There are exempt amounts, so you will receive some of your money, but it probably won't be enough to live on.

Like all types of levies, the IRS is required to first send you the Final Notice of Intent to Levy and Notice of Your Right to a Hearing. If this final notice is ignored, the IRS may levy your wages. When levying your wages, the IRS will send your employer *Form 668-W Notice of Levy*, and this form usually gives your employer at least one full pay period after receiving the Notice of Levy before they are required to send any funds to the IRS.

When your employer receives the Notice of Levy, they are required to give you a Statement of Dependents and Filing Status, and you are required to complete the form and return it to your employer within three days.[101] Upon receiving your Statement of Dependents and Filing Status, your employer will use Publication 1494 to compute the amounts exempt from levy. The exempt amounts are calculated with reference to your filing status and number of dependents you claim. All funds in excess of the exempt amount will be remitted to the IRS, and the levy will stay in place until your taxes are fully paid or it is released as a result of you making other arrangements (such as an Installment Agreement) with the IRS.

What to do if the IRS Levies Your Wages

If your wages are levied, you will need to call the IRS as soon as possible. There will be a number on your copy of the form that you will need to call. To ensure the best results, gather the following information for reference during your phone call:

1. Copy of the Notice of Levy.
2. Print *Form 433-F, Collection Information Statement* and pencil in the numbers if you have the information available. You don't have much time, so if you are unable to do this, you can proceed without it.
3. Your employer's telephone number to facilitate a levy release.
4. Your employer's fax number to facilitate a levy release.
5. Your payroll contact information to facilitate a levy release.

Your goal is to get the levy released quickly. If you are unable to pay the tax in full, the best alternative is to negotiate an Installment Agreement with the representative. If your circumstances dictate, you may be able to negotiate a Currently Not Collectible status. If the levy will cause a financial hardship, explain that to the representative. Your goal should be to take care of all of this during the phone call you initially make to the IRS, so if possible, have your information available before you call.

Levy on Bank Accounts

When the IRS decides to levy your assets, they will typically start with a bank levy and/or wage levy (garnishment). Wage levies are continuous, meaning they continue until the levy is released. Bank levies, on the other hand, are one and done.

While a revenue officer may hand deliver a bank levy, most bank levies are initiated by the IRS mailing the Notice of Levy to the bank.[102] The levy applies to all funds in the account, up to the total amount due, at the time of receipt of the levy by the bank. However, the levy does not apply to deposits made after the levy was received. For example, if you owe the IRS $10,000 and when the levy is received by the bank, you have $1,500 on deposit. Thereafter, you make a $500 deposit. The $1,500 in the account at the time of receipt of the levy will be frozen. The $500 deposit made later will remain untouched.

The IRS can serve the *Form 668-A, Notice of Levy* on the bank by mail, fax, or in person. It is the IRS policy to delay sending the taxpayer a copy of the levy for a long enough period that the bank has the opportunity to freeze the funds prior to you obtaining knowledge of the levy.[103] This prevents you from withdrawing the money before the levy can take place. When the levy is served, the bank will freeze the funds in your account (up to the total amount owed). However, the bank will not remit the funds to the IRS for 21 days.[104] This waiting period allows you time to notify the IRS if the levy was in error or make arrangements with the IRS to resolve your account.

What to Do If the IRS has Levied Your Bank Account

Once you receive your copy of the bank levy, or sooner if your bank notifies you, you need to call the IRS as quickly as possible. You must realize that your chances of getting the levy released are better if the money has not yet been sent to the IRS. Therefore, be prepared to enter into an Installment Agreement, Currently Not Collectible status, or other resolution during your call. You will need to provide detailed financial information during your call, so prepare accordingly. Your copy of the levy will have a phone number for you to call. For best results, have the following information available when you call:

1. Copy of the Notice of Levy.

2. Print *Form 433-F, Collection Information Statement* and pencil in the numbers if you have the information available. If time does not allow, you can call without this form being completed.

3. Your bank's telephone number to facilitate a levy release.

4. Your bank's fax number to facilitate a levy release.

5. Your bank contact information to facilitate a levy release.

6. Your account number.

Levy of your Personal or Real Property

It is very common for the IRS to levy wages, bank accounts, and investment accounts. It is quick and easy, and it avoids personal confrontations with taxpayers. It is relatively uncommon for the IRS to levy your personal or real property. If your property has been seized, the IRS likely tried the other avenues of collection without any luck.

There are some extra safeguards for levies of non-financial assets. For instance, the seizure of assets used in your trade or business requires the written approval of the Area Director or Assistant Area Director (IRS executives). In the case of a residence, not only must the Area Director approve the seizure, but the IRS must obtain a court order before seizing:[105]

- Your principal residence

- Your spouse's principal residence

- Your former spouse's principal residence

- The principal residence of your minor child.

Other properties are not subject to these same safeguards. If your property is seized, you should immediately contact the IRS to resolve your tax liability and request a levy release. If it is determined that the seizure is causing an immediate economic hardship, the IRS must release the levy. You may use the Collection Appeal Program to appeal a seizure before or after it has taken place, but it must be made prior to the property being sold. Prior to being sold at a public auction or sealed bid auction, the IRS will calculate a minimum bid price and provide you a copy of the calculation. You will have an opportunity to challenge the determination of the IRS. The IRS generally gives 10 days' notice prior to a sale, and unless you can reach an agreement with the IRS, your property will be sold and the net proceeds will be applied to your account.

If the IRS seizes and sells your real estate, you (or anybody with an interest in the property, including lienholders) can redeem the property within 180 days of the sale.[106] That means that, within 180 days, you can pay the purchaser the purchase price plus interest at 20% annually to redeem the property.

Jeopardy Levy

Despite all of the procedural hurdles the IRS must jump to levy your assets, there are circumstances in which the IRS can bypass many of these procedures and issue a levy immediately.[107] This is called a jeopardy levy. The conditions that allow a jeopardy levy are:[108]

1. You are or appear to be planning to quickly depart from the United States or to conceal yourself.

2. You are or appear to be planning to place your property beyond the reach of the IRS by removing it from the United States, by concealing it, by dissipating it, or by transferring it to other persons.

3. Your financial solvency appears to be imperiled (this insolvency is to be independent of insolvency caused by the assessment or collection of tax).

4. You are in possession of over $10,000 in cash and claim it is not yours or that it belongs to another specified person. The collection of tax on said cash is presumed to be in jeopardy. [109]

In non-jeopardy cases, you have the right to an appeal hearing prior to the levy. In the case of jeopardy levies, the levy is immediate with little or no notice. Therefore, with jeopardy levies, you have the right to appeal the levy after it has taken place. Within five days of the jeopardy levy, the IRS must provide a statement of information upon which they relied in making the levy.[110] The IRS will provide you with the appeals mechanisms available depending upon the timing of the notice. As with all IRS appeals, the time periods are strictly enforced, so a prompt appeal is necessary. If The Office of Independent Appeals issues a finding against you, there is a right to a judicial review. Due to a judicial review's tight time frames and complexity, tax counsel is recommended if you choose this course of action.

IRS Liability if Erroneous Levy Issued; Bank Fees

If the IRS levied your account in error and you were forced to pay fees to your bank as a result (including overdraft charges that are a direct consequence of the IRS error), you can complete and file *Form 8546, Claim for Reimbursement of Bank Charges*. For a valid claim, the following three conditions must be present:

1. The IRS acknowledges the levy was in error.

2. The taxpayer must not have contributed to the continuation or compounding of the error.

3. Prior to the levy, you did not refuse, either orally or in writing, to timely respond to IRS inquiries or provide information relevant to the liability for which the levy was made.

Form 8546 can also be used to make a claim against the IRS for costs incurred if they mistakenly debit your account or if you incur charges for stopping payment on a check submitted to the IRS that was lost by the IRS.

IRS Forms and Publications Related to This Chapter:

*   *Form 668-A – Notice of Levy*

*   *Form 668-W – Notice of Levy on Wages, Salary, and Other Income*

*   *Form 433-F – Collection Information Statement*

*   *Form 8546 - Claim for Reimbursement of Bank Charges*

*   *Publication 1660 – Collection Appeal Rights*

*   *Form 9423 – Collection Appeal Request*

*   *Form 12153 – Request for Collection Due Process or Equivalent Hearing*

CHAPTER 12:

Federal Tax Liens

A tax lien is a powerful tool used by the government to secure its claim when an individual or business owes unpaid taxes. In 2023, the IRS filed 179,019 Notices of Federal Tax Lien.[111] The filing of a lien significantly increases the likelihood that the IRS will collect the taxes.

For lien information or questions you can call the IRS Lien Desk directly at 800-913-6050.

What is a Lien?

A lien is a legal claim or right against an asset to secure the payment of a debt or other obligation. Liens are used to protect the interest of creditors who are owed money. Common examples of liens are your home mortgage, which must be fully paid to sell your house, or a finance lien on your car, which encumbers the transfer of your car until it is fully paid. When a lien is recorded at the county recorder's office, it becomes a matter of public record and is visible to anybody who searches the public record database. The filing of a Notice of Federal Tax Lien (NFTL) puts the public on notice that the IRS has a claim on and attaches to all of your existing property interests and property rights that you may acquire in the future.

Distinction Between a Federal Tax Lien and a Notice of Federal Tax Lien

A *Federal Tax Lien* against all your property arises once the tax has been assessed and demand for payment has been made (sometimes called a "Statutory Lien").[112] However, only the IRS knows about this lien, and because it is not a matter of public record, nobody else is bound by it. That all changes with the filing of a *Notice of Federal Tax Lien (NFTL)*.

Filing of Notice of Federal Tax Lien

If you fail to pay your tax after receiving a Notice and Demand for Payment, the IRS may file a Notice of Federal Tax Lien (NFTL). The IRS does this by sending the NFTL to the county recorder in your county of residence and any other counties where you own property (if the IRS is aware of the property). The recorded NFTL alerts creditors and potential buyers that the IRS has a legal claim against any property you have or may acquire in the future. If you receive a notice that the IRS has filed, or intends to file a Notice of Federal Tax Lien, be sure to explore your appeal options outlined in the Appeals chapter.

Balance Thresholds for Filing a Notice of Federal Tax Lien

Generally, you must owe $10,000 or more before the IRS will file a NFTL.[113] However, if you qualify for a Guaranteed Installment Agreement, Streamlined Installment Agreement, or In-Business Trust Fund Express Agreement, the IRS will generally not file a NFTL.[114]

Effect of a Filed Notice of Federal Tax Lien

The filing of a NFTL will create a public notice of the existence of the tax lien. The NFTL will show the balance of taxes, interest and penalties assessed as of the date of filing, but it is not updated as the balance is reduced, nor is it updated to account for additional penalties or interest.

The NFTL attaches to all of your property, but the most common issue you will face is the prevention of the sale or refinance of your real estate without paying the debt in full (after which the IRS will release the Federal Tax Lien) or otherwise addressing the lien through withdrawal, discharge, or subordination. Although the lien attaches to all of your property, there are some exceptions outlined in Internal Revenue Code § 6323. Without these exceptions, commerce would come to a screeching halt as everybody would have to search for liens before every transaction. The exceptions are:

1. Securities (stocks and bonds) as long as the purchaser did not know about the lien.

2. Motor vehicles so long as the purchaser did not know about the lien.

3. Tangible personal property purchased at retail from a seller in the ordinary course of seller's business, unless the purchaser knows or intends such purchase to hinder, evade or defeat the collection of tax.

4. Casual purchases of household goods listed in Internal Revenue Code §6334(a) for less than $1,000 as long as the purchaser does not know of the lien or that the sale is one of a series of sales.

5. Personal property subject to a possessory lien (such as a mechanic's lien for work on your car).

6. Property tax and special assessment liens.

7. Mechanic's liens on an owner's residence with an upper limit of $5,000.

8. Attorney's liens.

9. Certain insurance contracts.

10. Deposit secured loans.

Tax Liens and Your Credit

Historically, taxpayers were concerned about how the NFTL would affect their credit rating. This turned out to be good leverage for the IRS because a threat to file the NFTL would incentivize the taxpayer to pay the tax or otherwise arrange for payments so that a lien would not be filed. However it has been reported that starting in 2018, the major credit reporting agencies removed NFTLs from their credit reports.[115] For many taxpayers this has reduced the impact of having a NFTL filed. Lenders, however, may search public records for any recorded liens.

Will a Federal Tax Lien prevent you from getting a loan to purchase a house or car?

You can obtain a mortgage to buy a house or a secured loan to purchase personal property if you have a NFTL. It is the official position of the IRS that a Purchase Money Mortgage or a Purchase Money Security Interest, given in good faith to secure a loan for the purchase of real property or goods, has priority over an already recorded Notice of Federal Tax Lien.[116] I am aware of a number of my clients with seriously delinquent tax debt who have purchased new homes, RVs, vehicles, and other items that are secured by a Purchase Money Mortgage or Purchase Money Security Interest. These clients had previously recorded NFTLs. According to all of the rules we discussed, the security interests should be junior to the already filed NFTL.

However, based upon Revenue Ruling 68-57, the IRS will treat their lien as a junior lien under these circumstances.

Appeal of Notice of Federal Tax Lien

If the IRS informs you that they will or have filed a NFTL, you have the right to appeal using the Collection Due Process appeal program discussed in detail in the chapter entitled "Appeals." You may also appeal the denial of a withdrawal, release, discharge, or subordination.

How to Deal with a Notice of Federal Tax Lien

Other than an initial appeal of the filing of a NFTL, there are four ways to address the filed lien:

- Release of Federal Tax Lien
- Withdrawal of Notice of Federal Tax Lien
- Discharge of Property from Federal Tax Lien
- Subordination of Federal Tax Lien

Release of Federal Tax Lien

A release of the Federal Tax Lien will be filed by the IRS once your tax liability is fully paid, becomes legally unenforceable (as when the Collection Statute Expiration Date has expired), the IRS accepts a bond for payment of the liability or you have satisfied the payment terms of an accepted Offer in Compromise. This release is accomplished by the IRS filing a Certificate of Release of Federal Tax Lien in each county where the IRS has recorded a Notice of Federal Tax Lien.

How to Request a Certificate of Release of Federal Tax Lien

The IRS has 30 days to release your lien after you have satisfied your liability.[117] You will receive a copy of the lien release at your last known address. If the lien is not released within 30 days, you can request a Certificate of Release of Federal Tax Lien by writing the Collection Advisory Group a request that contains the following information:

- The date of your request.
- Name and address of taxpayer.
- Taxpayer's telephone number and best time to be reached.
- A copy of the NFTL taxpayer is requesting to be released.
- If applicable, canceled check or proof of payment.

This request must be sent to the Collection Advisory Group servicing your area. You can find the address of your Collection Advisory Group in *IRS Publication 4235.* Questions can be directed to Centralized Lien Operation at 800-913-6050 (Fax 855-753-8177). If you have an immediate need for a Certificate of Release of Federal Tax Lien, you will need to visit your local IRS office with all of your available documentation and proof of payment, if applicable.

Effect of Release of Federal Tax Lien

A release of the Federal Tax Lien clears your assets from the encumbrance of the lien. The public records will show a Notice of Federal Tax Lien, but there will be a corresponding document that reverses the effect of the lien.

Withdrawal of Notice of Federal Tax Lien

A withdrawal of a NFTL is a legal action by the IRS to remove the NFTL from the public record, and, therefore, the provisions of the Internal Revenue Code shall be applied as if the withdrawn notice had not been filed. The circumstances under which the IRS will withdraw a filed NFTL are: [118]

1. The filing of the Notice of Federal Tax Lien was premature or otherwise not in accordance with the IRS's administrative procedures.
2. You have entered into an Installment Agreement pursuant to IRC Section 6159 to satisfy the liability for which the lien was imposed and the terms of the agreement do not provide for a Notice of Federal Tax Lien to be filed.
3. The withdrawal will facilitate the collection of the tax liability.

4. With your consent or the National Taxpayer Advocate, the withdrawal of the Notice of Federal Tax Lien would be in the best interests of the taxpayer (as determined by the National Taxpayer Advocate) and the United States.

How to Apply for Withdrawal of Notice of Federal Tax Lien

To request a Withdrawal of Notice of Federal Tax Lien, submit an application for withdrawal on *Form 12277, Application for Withdrawal of Filed Notice of Federal Tax Lien.* Complete this form with your information, a copy of the NFTL (or serial number if a copy of the notice is not available), the basis for withdrawal (one of the circumstances listed above), and an explanation of the facts supporting the basis for withdrawal. This form is submitted to the Advisory Group Manager in the area where you live. The address for submission based upon your address can be found in *Publication 4235, Advisory Group Addresses.* If your *Application for Withdrawal of Notice of Federal Tax Lien* is denied, you can appeal by following the directions in your denial notice.

Special Notice: Upon your written request, the IRS will notify other interested parties of the withdrawal notice. Your request must be in writing, and you must list the names and addresses of creditors, credit reporting agencies, or financial institutions to which you want notifications to be sent. If, at a later date, you require further notifications, follow the specific instructions on *Form 12277, Application for Withdrawal of Filed Notice of Federal Tax Lien.*

Effect of a Withdrawal of Notice of Federal Tax Lien

The filing of a Withdrawal of Notice of Federal Tax Lien treats the notice as if it were never filed. It does not affect the underlying assessment lien or the underlying liability, but it will result in a loss of the IRS's priority over other creditors.[119]

Discharge of Property from a Federal Tax Lien

Are you trying to sell a property encumbered by an NFTL? A discharge is your solution. Unlike a withdrawal or release, a discharge applies only to a specific property, leaving the NFTL in place for all other property. Here is an example:

You own a house worth $500,000. There is a first mortgage of $400,000 that was recorded when you purchased the house on January 1, 2023. You took out a second mortgage (also known as a home equity loan) in the amount of $60,000, which was recorded on June 1, 2023. On July 1, the IRS recorded an NFTL in the amount of $750,000 for a tax liability from the past. On December 1, 2023, you sell the house for $600,000. Your sale numbers will look like this:

$600,000 sales price

$500,000 first mortgage

$60,000 second mortgage

$37,000 expenses of sale, such as commission, title insurance, escrow, etc. (Using an approximation for purposes of illustration).

$3,000 equity after bona fide expenses of sale.

The IRS has a security interest in the equity by virtue of its NFTL. However, there is a $750,000 NFTL, so normally, the title insurance/escrow company/closing attorney will not be able to close unless the entire $750,000 is paid, satisfying the lien. This is where a discharge comes in. In this case, you can complete and submit *Form 14135, Application for Certificate of Discharge of Property from Federal Tax Lien.*

In our example, the two mortgages were recorded before the NFTL; therefore, they are considered "senior" to the NFTL and are not affected by the lien. The IRS will allow bona fide expenses of sale. After the senior liens and expenses of sale, $3,000 in equity remains. That constitutes the IRS's interest in the property. In this case, the IRS will discharge this property in exchange for the $3,000 in equity and allow the transaction to close. The IRS will coordinate with the escrow company or closing attorney to arrange for closing with instructions to remit the $3,000 in equity directly to the IRS.

The above example is the most common use of discharge, but there are five different scenarios where a discharge may be granted:

1. If there are multiple properties encumbered by the NFTL, the IRS may discharge a particular property if the equity in the remaining properties is at least double the liability covered by the NFTL. See IRC Section 6325(b)(1).

2. The IRS receives an amount not less than the government's interest. In our example, above, the government's interest was $3,000. So long as they receive the government's interest, they will discharge the property. See IRC Section 6325(b)(2)(A).

3. The interest of the IRS in the property to be discharged has no value. In our example, if, after payment of the senior mortgages and bona fide costs of sale, there was no equity, the IRS would discharge the property because there was no value in the IRS's interest in the property. See IRC Section 6325(b)(2)(B).

4. The IRS may discharge the property if, pursuant to an agreement with the IRS, proceeds from the sale are held in escrow subject to the NFTL and claims of the United States. See IRC Section 6325(b)(3).

5. The IRS may discharge the property if a deposit is made or a bond is furnished in an amount equal to the United States' interest. In our example, above, the deposit would be in the amount of $3,000.

How to Apply for Discharge of Property from Federal Tax Lien

To apply for a discharge, complete and submit *Form 14135, Application for Certificate of Discharge of Property from Federal Tax Lien*. The form asks detailed questions and requires the submission of supporting documents. The information required includes:

- Identification of the parties to the transaction.
- Identification of lender and escrow company.
- Basis of discharge (which code section applies to this transaction – see sections referenced above).
- Description of the property, including deed with legal description.
- Property appraisal by a disinterested third party.
- Copy or copies of the NFTL or lien numbers of NFTLs that encumber the property.
- Purchase agreement, title report, and proposed settlement statement.

Once the application is submitted, it takes approximately 45 days to process. This is longer than the typical real estate escrow. When requested, the IRS will try to expedite its review to meet your deadlines, although you should not count on them to finish their review early.

Effect of Discharge of Property from Federal Tax Lien

The effect of a discharge of property from a Federal Tax Lien is the removal of the Federal Tax Lien from a specific property. This allows you to sell or refinance that particular property. However, it is important to note that the lien remains attached to all other property and future rights to your property. The discharge does not eliminate the Federal Tax Lien from the rest of your property.

Little Known Benefit; Help with Moving Expenses

If you are selling your principal residence and are requesting a discharge under IRC Section 6325(b)(2)(A) (the IRS receives no less than the government's interest) you can request an allowance for moving expenses. To do so, you must complete *Form 12451, Request for Relocation Expenses Allowance.* Ideally, this document should be submitted with your *Form 14135, Application for Certificate of Discharge of Property from Federal Tax Lien. The Request for Relocation Expenses Allowance* is a one-page, simple, self-explanatory document. However, there are two sections which require particular attention to detail.

Section 6 of Form 12451 (Request for Relocation Expenses Allowance)

This section outlines the "amount of relocation expenses requested (please provide sufficient documentation to support requested expenses)." In this section, enter each item of expense reimbursement requested, along with written substantiation to support the request. For instance, for costs related to professional movers, provide a copy of a written quote from the moving company. If you can provide two quotes from two different companies, that would be even better. If requesting mileage reimbursement, attach a printed map along with the mileage reimbursement requested. The more documentation you can provide for each entry in this section, the more likely your request will be approved without delay. Remember, you will be on a tight timeline to get this approved in time to close escrow on your property.

Section 7 of Form 12451 (Request for Relocation Expenses Allowance)

This section states, "Please explain your financial circumstances and provide supporting documentation." Writing something like, "My necessary living expenses equal or exceed my monthly income, so I will not have any money to move to my new personal residence" will not cut it. Instead, attach a completed and signed *Form 433-F, Collection Information Statement* and documentation for the significant income and expense items. Include a month's worth of pay stubs, three months of your bank statements, copies of bills for your largest expenses (rent, utilities, car payments, insurance payments, etc.), and any other information that will shed light on your financial situation. Remember - provide as much information and documentation as practical. If the information is not included and the IRS has to contact you to obtain further information, that will delay the approval and delay the closing of your real estate transaction.

Subordination of Federal Tax Lien

To understand how a subordination works and when you would need to use it, first, let's examine how liens and their priorities work. Typically, with larger loans, creditors take a security interest in your property. The most common examples are home mortgages and car loans. In both cases, the lenders take a security interest in the collateral (the property used to ensure payment) by creating a lien. If there is a lien on your property from your lender and you don't make the payments as promised, the lender can foreclose on the property against which the lien is recorded.

More than one lender can have a security interest in the same property, but their security interests are ranked according to priority. Priority results from recording your lien (in the case of a house, this is recorded in the County Recorder's office) before the other lender records his. The lender who had recorded his lien first will have priority over a subsequent lender (or lenders) and will be paid first from the proceeds of a foreclosure on the property.

If there is a recorded Notice of Federal Tax Lien, that lien will take priority over liens securing any loans you receive after the NFTL has been recorded. Lenders may not wish to give you a second mortgage loan or refinance a first mortgage loan because their security interest will be inferior to the IRS tax lien interest. If their interest is behind the IRS, if the property were to go into foreclosure, the IRS would be paid first. This is where subordination comes into play. In the context of federal tax liens, a subordination is an agreement with the IRS that lets another creditor be higher in priority than the tax lien, even though the tax lien was recorded first. The Notice of Federal Tax Lien will still be an encumbrance on the property, but it will have a lower priority than the new lender's lien. Here is an example that illustrates how subordination works:

A taxpayer purchases a $100,000 home with a down payment of $20,000 and a loan of $80,000. At a date after the purchase of the home, the IRS files an NFTL in the amount of $20,000. The prevailing interest rates for home loans fell to a point where the taxpayer could save on his monthly payments by refinancing his loan. However, the new loan will be secured by a mortgage that is recorded after the date of the recording of the NFTL. That would mean the tax lien was senior to the mortgage, and in the event of foreclosure, the tax lien would be paid first. This is not something the lender will allow. This is where subordination comes in. The taxpayer can ask the IRS to subordinate their lien to the new mortgage. Such a subordination would not make the lien go away; it is just an agreement by the IRS to consider their NFTL junior to the new mortgage. This has the same legal effect as if the mortgage was recorded first and the NFTL was recorded second.

Basis for Subordination

The IRS, however, does not agree to subordination without getting something in return. A subordination can be granted upon one of two bases.

First, a subordination may be granted if the subordination includes a payment to the IRS of the equity obtained from your refinanced loan after paying off the existing loan.[120] In our example above, if the $80,000 loan was refinanced for $90,000, the IRS would demand the $10,000 in equity refinanced after paying off the $80,000 loan.

Second, a subordination may be granted if the IRS determines the approval of the subordination will increase the amount the government realizes and make collection of the tax liability easier for the IRS.[121] A commonly occurring example of this is if the refinance reduced the monthly mortgage payment thereby allowing a larger monthly payment by the taxpayer toward the existing tax liability.

How to Apply for a Subordination of Federal Tax Lien

The subordination process begins by filing *Form 14134, Application for Certificate of Subordination of Federal Tax Lien* along with the supporting documents required by the IRS. This application requires the following information:

- Your name, address, phone, social security number, etc.
- Applicant information, if different from the taxpayer.

- Property owner.

- Attorney/representative contact information.

- Lender.

- Old and new loan amounts.

- Basis of subordination

  - 6325(d)(1) - IRS receives refinanced equity.

  - 6325(d)(2) - IRS interest increased, and collection of tax is made easier.

- Description of property.

- Address of property, including legal description, if applicable.

- Appraisal and valuations

  - A disinterested 3rd party appraisal is required, along with:

    - County valuation of real property (located on your property tax bill).

    - Informal valuation by disinterested 3rd party.

    - Proposed selling price for property to be sold at auction.

- Copy of NFTL or the lien number if copies of the NFTL are unavailable.

- Copy of proposed loan agreement.

- Description of how subordination is in the interest of the United States.

  - In this section, explain how the IRS will receive higher monthly payments or how the IRS will receive some sort of payment along with the subordination.

- Copy of current preliminary title report (for real property).

- Copy of proposed closing statement (sometimes called a settlement statement). This shows all of the figures related to the refinance or subordination.

- Additional information that may have a bearing on the request.

As of this writing it takes a minimum of 45 days to complete a subordination. It is important to let your lender and other involved parties know of the extended review period so that accommodations can be made by the various parties involved.

Effect of Subordination of Federal Tax Lien

If the IRS agrees to subordinate its NFTL, it allows the subject lien to be considered to have priority over the NFTL. It will be treated as if it were recorded before the NFTL. This subordination is specific to the identified NFTL in the subordination documents and does not affect any other liens. The tax liability itself will not be changed by the subordination.

IRS Forms and Publications Related to This Chapter:

- *Form 668(Y), Notice of Federal Tax Lien*

- *Publication 1468 – Guidelines for Notices of Federal Tax Liens and Centralized Lien Processing*

- *Publication 783 – How to Apply for a Certificate of Discharge From Federal Tax Lien*

- *Form 14135 – Application for Certificate of Discharge of Property from Federal Tax Lien*

- *Form 12451 – Request for Relocation Expenses Allowance*

- *Publication 784 – Instructions on How to Apply for a Certificate of Subordination of Federal Tax Lien*

- *Form 14134 – Application for Certificate of Subordination of Federal Tax Lien*

- *Publication 1024 – How to Prepare Application for Certificate of Nonattachment of Federal Tax Lien*

- *Publication 1450 – Instructions for Requesting a Certificate of Release of Federal Tax Lien*

- *Form 12277 – Application for Withdrawal of Filed Form 668(Y), Notice of Federal Tax Lien*

- *Publication 4235 – Collection Advisory Offices Contact Information (who to call for lien related certificates)*

- *Form 433-F – Collection Information Statement*

- *Form 433-A – Collection Information Statement for Wage Earners and Self-Employed Individuals*

- *Form 433-B - Collection Information Statement for Businesses*

- *Publication 1660 – Collection Appeal Rights*

- *Form 9423 – Collection Appeal Request*

- *Form 12153 – Request for Collection Due Process or Equivalent Hearing*

CHAPTER 13:

Innocent Spouse Relief

The innocent spouse provisions of the Internal Revenue Code are safeguards designed to offer relief to individuals who find themselves unfairly burdened by their spouse's or former spouse's understatement of tax. Below, we examine the different avenues of relief tailored to different circumstances in which an innocent spouse might be unjustly encumbered for taxes and penalties without any fault of their own.[122]

There are four main categories of innocent spouse relief, each of which we will examine in order:

1. Innocent Spouse Relief for All Joint Filers (IRC 6015(b));

2. Innocent Spouse Relief for Taxpayers No Longer Married or Taxpayers Legally Separated or Not Living Together. This is also known as "Separation of Liability Relief" (IRC 6015(c)).

3. Innocent Spouse Relief - Equitable Relief (IRC 6015(f));

4. Relief from Liability for Tax Attributable to Item of Community Income (Internal Revenue Code Section 66(c)). This only applies to a spouse in a community property state (AZ, CA, ID, LA, NV, NM, TX, WA, and WI).

The following flowchart contained in IRS Publication 971 gives an overview of the qualifications for Innocent Spouse Relief.

Flowcharts

The following flowcharts provide a quick way for determining whether you may qualify for relief. But do not rely on these flowcharts alone. Also read the earlier discussions.

Figure A. Do You Qualify for Innocent Spouse Relief?

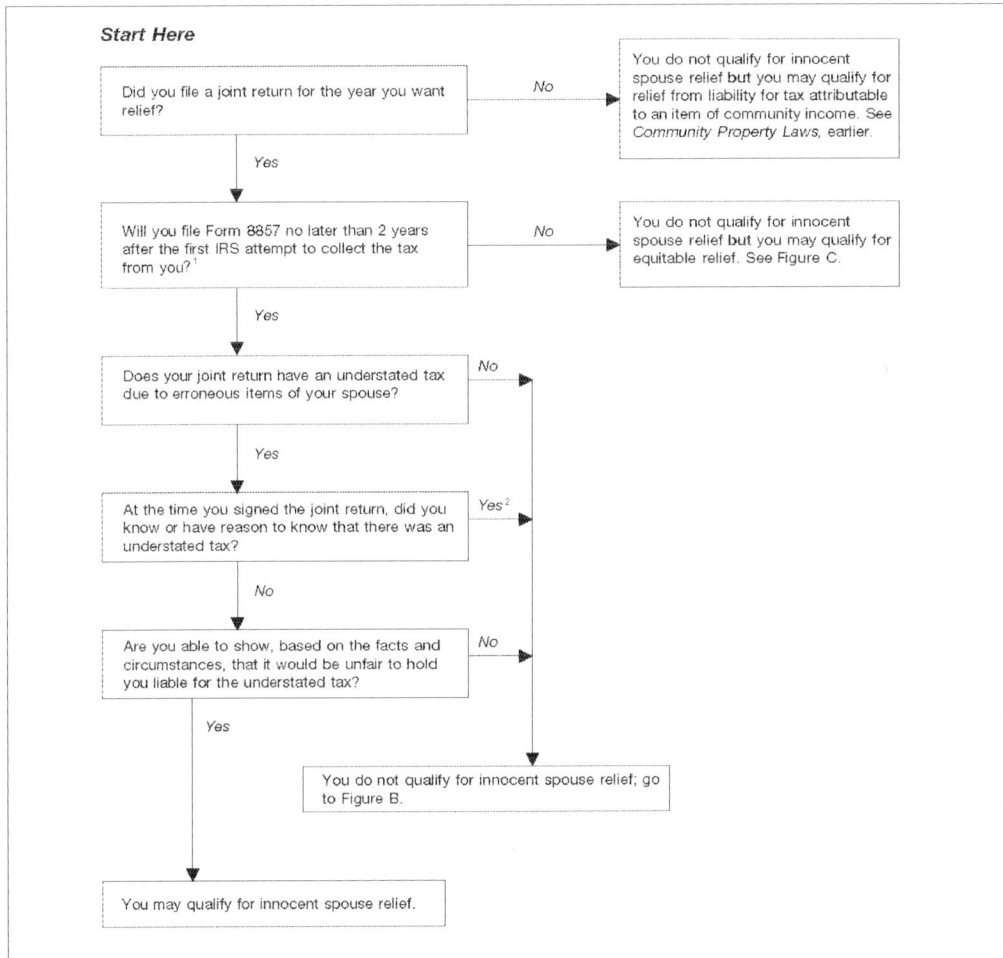

Start Here

Did you file a joint return for the year you want relief? — **No** → You do not qualify for innocent spouse relief but you may qualify for relief from liability for tax attributable to an item of community income. See *Community Property Laws,* earlier.

↓ **Yes**

Will you file Form 8857 no later than 2 years after the first IRS attempt to collect the tax from you?[1] — **No** → You do not qualify for innocent spouse relief but you may qualify for equitable relief. See Figure C.

↓ **Yes**

Does your joint return have an understated tax due to erroneous items of your spouse? — **No** →

↓ **Yes**

At the time you signed the joint return, did you know or have reason to know that there was an understated tax? — **Yes**[2] →

↓ **No**

Are you able to show, based on the facts and circumstances, that it would be unfair to hold you liable for the understated tax? — **No** →

↓ **Yes**

You do not qualify for innocent spouse relief; go to Figure B.

↓

You may qualify for innocent spouse relief.

[1] Collection activities that may start the 2-year period are described earlier under *How To Request Relief.*

[2] You may qualify for partial relief if, at the time you filed your return, you knew or had reason to know of only a portion of an erroneous item.

Publication 971 (December 2021)

Figure B. Do You Qualify for Separation of Liability Relief?

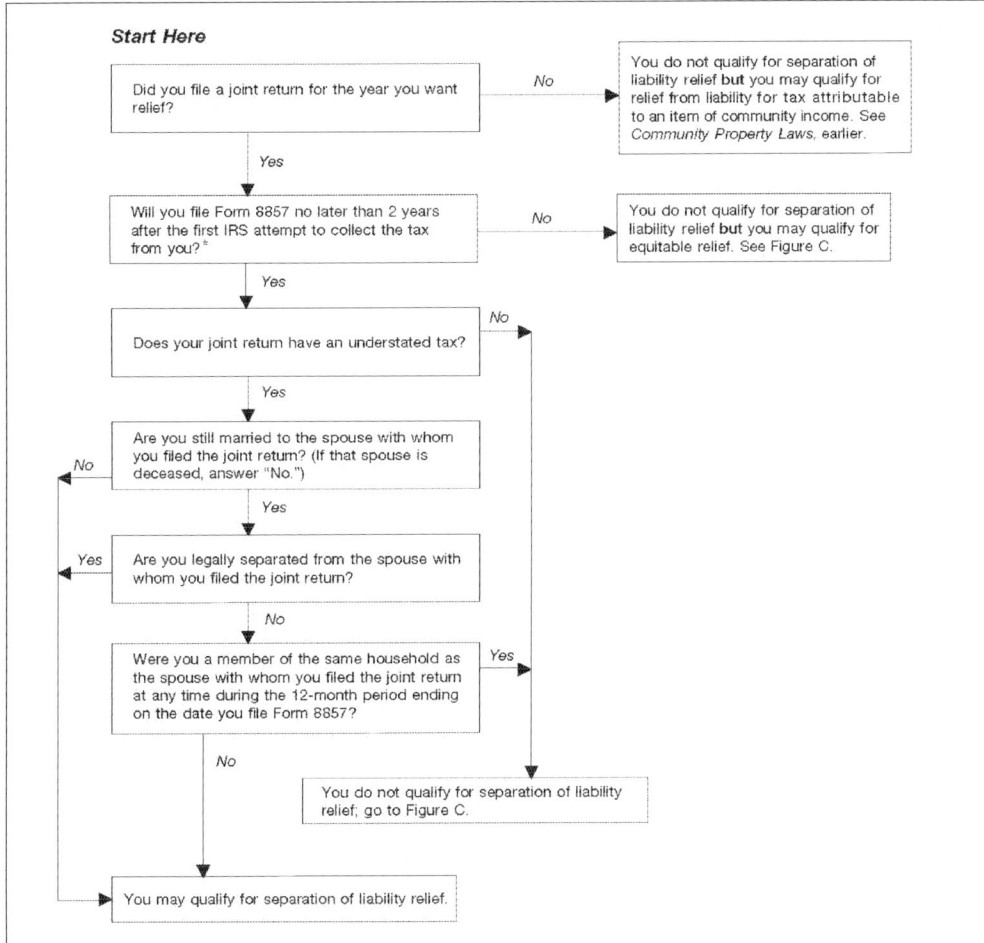

Start Here

Did you file a joint return for the year you want relief?

→ **No** → You do not qualify for separation of liability relief **but** you may qualify for relief from liability for tax attributable to an item of community income. See *Community Property Laws*, earlier.

↓ *Yes*

Will you file Form 8857 no later than 2 years after the first IRS attempt to collect the tax from you?*

→ **No** → You do not qualify for separation of liability relief **but** you may qualify for equitable relief. See Figure C.

↓ *Yes*

Does your joint return have an understated tax?

→ *No* ↓

↓ *Yes*

Are you still married to the spouse with whom you filed the joint return? (If that spouse is deceased, answer "No.")

→ *No* →

↓ *Yes*

Are you legally separated from the spouse with whom you filed the joint return?

→ *Yes* →

↓ *No*

Were you a member of the same household as the spouse with whom you filed the joint return at any time during the 12-month period ending on the date you file Form 8857?

→ *Yes* ↓

↓ *No*

You do not qualify for separation of liability relief; go to Figure C.

You may qualify for separation of liability relief.

*Collection activities that may start the 2-year period are described earlier under *How To Request Relief*.

Publication 971 (December 2021)

Figure C. Do You Qualify for Equitable Relief?

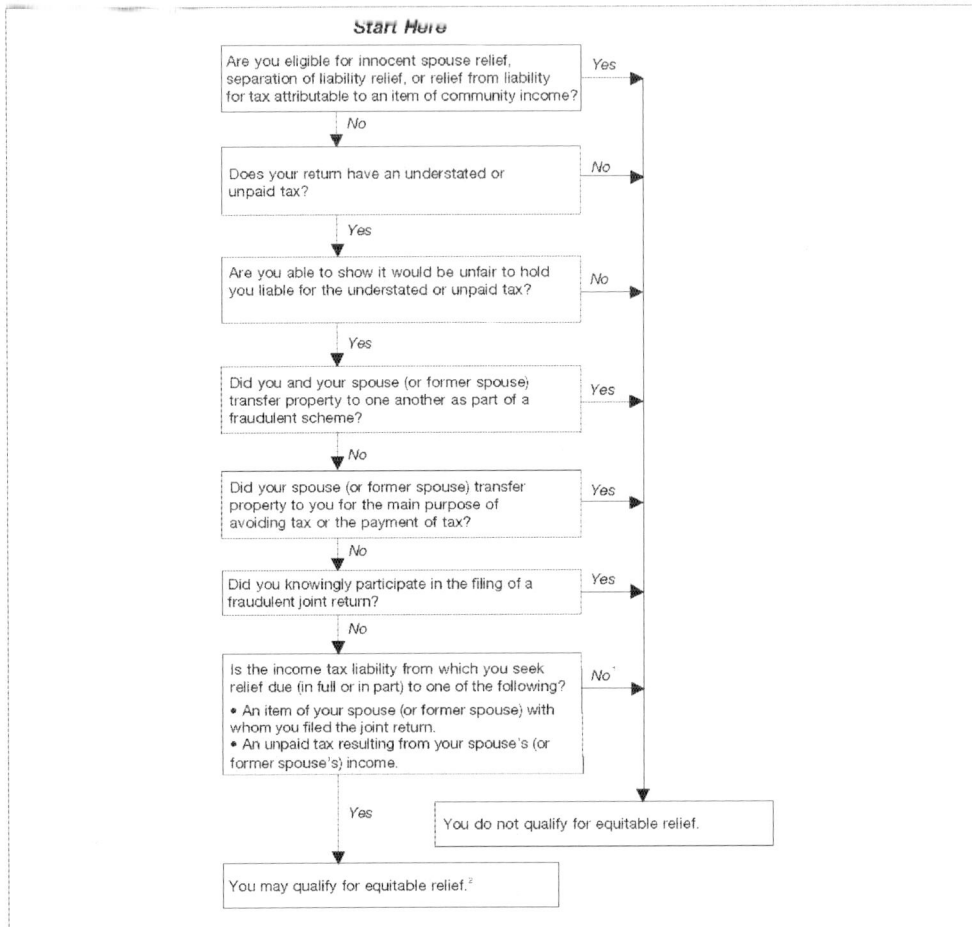

Start Here

Are you eligible for innocent spouse relief, separation of liability relief, or relief from liability for tax attributable to an item of community income? — **Yes** →

↓ **No**

Does your return have an understated or unpaid tax? — **No** →

↓ **Yes**

Are you able to show it would be unfair to hold you liable for the understated or unpaid tax? — **No** →

↓ **Yes**

Did you and your spouse (or former spouse) transfer property to one another as part of a fraudulent scheme? — **Yes** →

↓ **No**

Did your spouse (or former spouse) transfer property to you for the main purpose of avoiding tax or the payment of tax? — **Yes** →

↓ **No**

Did you knowingly participate in the filing of a fraudulent joint return? — **Yes** →

↓ **No**

Is the income tax liability from which you seek relief due (in full or in part) to one of the following? — **No** [1] →

• An item of your spouse (or former spouse) with whom you filed the joint return.
• An unpaid tax resulting from your spouse's (or former spouse's) income.

↓ **Yes**

→ **You do not qualify for equitable relief.**

You may qualify for equitable relief. [2]

[1] You may qualify for equitable relief if you meet any of the exceptions to condition (7) discussed earlier under *Conditions for Getting Equitable Relief.*
[2] You must file Form 8857 by the filing deadlines explained earlier in *Exception for equitable relief* under *How To Request Relief.*

Publication 971 (December 2021)

Innocent Spouse Relief; Procedures for Relief from Liability Applicable to All Joint Filers (IRC 6015(b))

Married taxpayers can elect to file their tax returns separately or jointly. There are some tax advantages to filing jointly. However, one drawback of filing jointly is that any tax liability is joint and several, meaning both parties owe the money (joint), and each individual party owes the money (several). Under these circumstances, the IRS can collect against either or both spouses. Under certain circumstances, this can lead to unfair results. For instance, if one spouse earned money without the other spouse's knowledge and failed to report the income, both spouses would be liable, even though one spouse was "innocent." Under the circumstances outlined in this section, the innocent spouse may be relieved of liability.

Necessary Elements

You can qualify for relief of all or a part of a joint tax liability if you can show the following:

1. You and your spouse filed a joint return.
2. The joint tax return contains an understatement of tax attributable to erroneous items of your spouse or former spouse.
3. At the time the return was filed, you did not know of or have reason to know of the understatement of tax.
4. Taking into consideration all the facts and circumstances, it would be unfair to hold you liable.
5. You request the relief within two years after collection activity is first taken against you.

Here are the conditions in a bit more detail:

Joint Return

You must have filed a joint return. Unlike married filing separately, when filing a joint return, each spouse is jointly and severally liable, and the IRS can collect against either or both spouses.

Understatement of Tax Attributable to Erroneous Items

An understatement of tax exists when the IRS determines that your total tax should be more than the amount that was shown on your joint return. Erroneous items include income received by your spouse that your spouse did not report. It can also include any improper deduction, credit, or property basis claimed by your spouse.

Actual Knowledge or Reason to Know

To qualify, you must <u>not</u> have actually known or had reason to know about the erroneous item. You are considered to have reason to know if a reasonable person in similar circumstances would have known about the understatement of tax. In determining if you had reason to know, the IRS will review all the facts and circumstances of the case, including:

- The nature of the erroneous item and the amount of the erroneous item relative to other items.
- The financial situation of you and your spouse.
- Your educational background and business experience.
- The extent of your participation in the activity that resulted in the erroneous item.
- Whether you failed to ask, at or before the time the return was signed, about items on the return or omitted from the return that a reasonable person would question.
- Whether the erroneous item represented a departure from a recurring pattern reflected in prior years' returns. An example of this would be omitted income from an investment regularly reported on prior years' returns.

Partial Relief

If you had no knowledge or reason to know of a portion of an erroneous item, you would be relieved of the understated tax due to that portion of the erroneous item if all the other requirements were met for that portion.[123] An example used by the IRS is as follows:

Requesting spouse knew of unreported gambling winnings of $5,000. After an audit, the IRS found that the unreported gambling winnings were actually $25,000. The requesting spouse established that he or she did not know and had no reason to know about the additional $20,000 because of the way the non-requesting spouse handled gambling winnings. Assuming all other requirements are met, the requesting spouse would be relieved of the $20,000 in additional gambling winnings but would not be relieved of the understatement due to the $5,000 of which the requesting spouse had knowledge.

Indications of Unfairness for Innocent Spouse Relief

The IRS will consider all of the facts and circumstances to determine whether it would be unfair to hold you liable for the understated tax. This is a subjective determination, but the IRS has outlined the following factors it will consider:

- Whether you received a significant benefit, directly or indirectly, from the understated tax. A significant benefit is a benefit in excess of normal support. What is normal support for one person might not be for another. Normal support for you is determined by your particular circumstances.

- Whether you were deserted by your spouse.

- Whether you and your spouse have been divorced or separated.

- Whether you received a benefit on the return from the understated tax.

How to Apply and Time Limits for Requesting Relief

You must make your request on *Form 8857, Request for Innocent Spouse Relief* within two years after the date the IRS first attempts to collect the tax from you. Collection activities that start the 2-year period include:

- IRS offset your income tax refund against an amount you owed on a joint return for another year, and the IRS informed you of your right to file *Form 8857.*

- The filing of a claim by the IRS in a court proceeding in which you were a party or the filing of a claim in a proceeding that involves your property. This includes the filing of a proof of claim on a bankruptcy proceeding.

- The filing of a suit by the US against you to collect the joint liability.

- The issuance of an IRC Section 6330 notice, which notifies you of the IRS's intent to levy and your right to a collections due process hearing. The IRS usually sends an IRC Section 6330 notice by issuing a Letter 11 or Letter 1058.

Procedures to Limit Liability for Taxpayers No Longer Married or Taxpayers Legally Separated or Not Living Together (IRC Section 6015(c))

Under this type of relief (also referred to as **Separation of Liability Relief**), the understated tax on the joint return is allocated between you and your spouse, each being solely responsible for your portion. If all or part of the application for relief is denied under IRC 6015(b), you may be able to obtain relief under this section for the amount that was denied.

Requirements for Relief under Section 6015(c)

1. A joint return was filed.

2. You and your spouse must no longer be married or must be legally separated (you are no longer married under this rule if you are widowed).

3. You and your spouse cannot have been members of the same household at any time during the 12-month period ending on the date the *Form 8857, Request for Innocent Spouse Relief* was filed. You and your spouse are considered members of the same household if <u>any</u> of the following conditions are met:

   a. You and your spouse reside in the same dwelling.

   b. You and your spouse reside in separate dwellings but are not estranged, and one of you is temporarily absent from the other's household.

   c. Either of you are temporarily absent from the household, and it is reasonable to assume that the absent spouse will return to the household. The household or a substantially equivalent household is maintained in anticipation of the absent spouse's return. Examples of temporary absences include those due to imprisonment, illness, business, vacation, military service, or education.

4. The IRS cannot show that you had actual knowledge, at the time the joint return was signed, of any item giving rise to the deficiency. Actual knowledge may not be disqualifying, however, in the case of domestic abuse or violence by your spouse.[124] In such a case, you must show that:

   a. You were a victim of domestic abuse before signing the return; and

b. You did not challenge the treatment of any items on the return for fear of retaliation by your spouse.

5. You must request relief by filing *Form 8857, Request for Innocent Spouse Relief* within two years of the IRS's first collection activities against you.

Limitations on Relief

Even if you qualify under the provisions of this section, relief will not be granted if:

1. The IRS proves that you and your spouse transferred assets to one another as part of a fraudulent scheme, including a scheme to defraud the IRS or another third party such as a creditor, former spouse, or business partner; or

2. Your spouse transferred property to you to avoid tax or the payment of tax. Unless the transfer was made under a divorce decree, separate maintenance agreement, or written instrument incident to such an agreement, a transfer will be presumed to be made in order to avoid tax if it was made within one year before the IRS sent its first letter of proposed deficiency.[125]

How to Apply and Time Limits for Requesting Relief

You must apply by submitting *Form 8857, Request for Innocent Spouse Relief* within two years after the date the IRS first attempts to collect the tax from you. Collection activities that start the two-year period include:

1. IRS offset your income tax refund against an amount you owed on a joint return for another year, and the IRS informed you of your right to file *Form 8857.*

2. The filing of a claim by the IRS in a court proceeding in which you were a party or the filing of a claim in a proceeding that involves your property. This includes the filing of a proof of claim on a bankruptcy proceeding.

3. The filing of a suit by the US against you to collect the joint liability.

4. The issuance of an IRC Section 6330 notice, which notifies you of the IRS's intent to levy and your right to a collections due process hearing. The IRS usually sends an IRC Section 6330 notice by issuing a Letter 11 or Letter 1058.

Innocent Spouse Relief; Equitable Relief (IRC Section 6015(f))

If you do not qualify for relief under Internal Revenue Code Section 6015(b) (Procedures for Relief from Liability Applicable to All Joint Filers) or Internal Revenue Code Section 6015(c) (Procedures to Limit Liability for Taxpayers no Longer Married or Taxpayers Legally Separated or Not Living Together) you may still qualify for relief.

Congress has provided the IRS the option of granting relief when other relief provisions do not apply.[126] If, taking into account all the facts and circumstances, it is inequitable to hold you liable for any unpaid tax or any deficiency, the IRS is allowed to relieve you of liability.

First, the IRS will examine whether you meet the "Threshold Requirements." If so, and if you meet the Streamlined Criteria[127] the IRS will grant relief. If you do not meet the Streamlined Criteria, the IRS will determine if you meet the equitable relief factors set forth in Revenue Procedure 2013-34.

Eligibility Threshold Requirements

The IRS will first determine if you meet the Eligibility Threshold Requirements.[128] They are:

1. **Joint Return** was filed for the year in which relief is filed.
2. **Neither IRC 6015(b) nor IRC 6015(c) provide relief**. (Procedures for relief from liability applicable to all joint filers and procedures to limit liability for taxpayers no longer married or taxpayers legally separated or not living together).
   a. Paragraphs 1 and 2 do not apply for relief under IRC 66(c) - Relief from Liability for Tax Attributable to Item of Community Income.
3. **Time Limitation**. You must apply for relief while the collection statute remains open (CSED is generally ten years from assessment). If part of the liability has been paid, you can request a refund if the refund statute is open (generally three years from the date the tax return was filed or two years after payment, whichever is later).
4. **No Fraudulent Transfers**. No relief will be granted if assets were transferred between you and your spouse as part of a fraudulent scheme to avoid tax or payment of tax.

5. **No Transfer of Disqualified Assets.** No relief will be granted to the extent of the value of disqualified assets that were transferred to you. A disqualified asset is any property transferred to you from your spouse in order to avoid tax or payment of tax. A transfer is presumed to be a disqualified asset if it was made during the 12-period period before the mailing date of the first letter of proposed deficiency or any time thereafter.[129] This rule does not apply if you did not have actual knowledge of the transfer or were abused or your spouse maintained control over finances by restricting your access to financial information.

6. **No Fraudulent Return.** You must not have knowingly participated in the filing of a fraudulent joint return.

7. **Attributable to the Non-Requesting Spouse.** Generally speaking, equitable relief will not be considered if the liability is solely attributable to you. If the liability is attributable to both you and your spouse, equitable relief will only be considered for the portion attributable to your spouse.[130]

If these Eligibility Threshold Requirements are met, the IRS will determine if the case meets the requirements of a Streamlined Determination.[131] If all of the following criteria are met, the relief will be granted under the Streamlined Determination:

1. You are no longer married to your spouse.

2. Economic hardship will result if relief is not granted.

3. You did not know or have reason to know of the understatement or that your spouse would not or could not pay the underpayment of tax.

Equitable Relief Factors

If relief cannot be granted due to failure of one of the Streamlined Determination criteria, the IRS must consider the equitable relief factors of Section 4.03 of Revenue Procedure 2013-34. The factors are designed as guides and they do not exclude other factors that may be present. The weight given to any factor depends on all the facts and circumstances of the case. The factors are as follows:[132]

1. **Marital Status.** This factor weighs in favor of relief if you and your spouse are no longer married, are legally separated, widowed, or have not been members of the same household for the previous 12 months.

2. **Economic Hardship**. If denying relief will cause you to suffer economic hardship, this factor will weigh in favor of relief. The IRS will consider your income, expenses, and assets to determine if economic hardship exists.

3. **Knowledge or Reason to Know**. This factor will weigh in favor of relief if:

   a. You did not know or have reason to know of the item giving rise to the understatement at the time you filed the joint return; or

   b. You had a reasonable expectation at the time the joint return was filed that your spouse would pay the liability at the time the return was filed or within a reasonable time thereafter.[133]

If you had actual knowledge or reason to know of the item, or if you could not reasonably expect that your spouse would or could pay the tax within a reasonable period of time, this factor will weigh against relief.

4. **Legal Obligation**. If your spouse has the sole legal obligation to pay the outstanding income tax liability pursuant to a divorce decree or agreement, this factor will weigh in favor of relief. If you have the sole legal obligation, this factor will weigh against relief.

5. **Significant Benefit**. This factor will weigh against relief if you enjoyed significant benefits (beyond normal support) such as living a lavish lifestyle, owning luxury assets, or taking expensive vacations. If you enjoyed little to no benefit and only your spouse significantly benefited, this factor will weigh in favor of relief.

6. **Compliance with Tax Laws**. This factor relates to your good faith effort to comply with the income tax laws in the taxable years following the period for which relief is requested.

   a. This factor will weigh in favor of relief if you:

      i. Are compliant for taxable years after being divorced from your spouse; or

      ii. Remain married to your spouse but file separate returns and are compliant with the tax laws.

   b. This factor will weigh against relief if you:

      i. Are not compliant for taxable years after being divorced from your spouse,

      ii. Remain married (whether or not legally separated or living apart) and continue to file joint returns after requesting relief and the returns are not compliant; or

      iii.   Remain married to your spouse, file separate returns, and are noncompliant with the tax laws.

7. **Mental or Physical Health**. This factor would weigh in favor of relief if you were in poor mental or physical health at the time you filed the returns or at the time you requested relief. The IRS will consider the nature, extent, and duration of the condition.

8. **Other Factors**. Other relevant factors on relief shall be considered.

If you are requesting Innocent Spouse Relief based on Equitable Factors, it is best to review the specifics of Revenue Procedure 2013-34 for a complete understanding of how the IRS will apply and interpret the different factors. This revenue procedure can be viewed at **IRS.gov/pub/irs-drop/rp-13-34.pdf**.

How to Apply and Time Limits for Requesting Relief

Use *Form 8857, Request for Innocent Spouse Relief.* The time limits for requesting equitable relief differ from the other types of relief requested. The time limits depend on whether you are requesting relief from a balance that you owe to the IRS or seeking a refund or credit.

If You Have a Balance Due

The IRS has, as a general rule, ten years to collect a balance from you. If you owe the IRS a balance and want to request equitable relief, you can do so at any time before the expiration of the Collection Statute Expiration Date (CSED). In other words, as long as the IRS has the legal authority to collect from you, you can request equitable relief.

If You Are Seeking a Refund or a Credit to Your Account

In this case, you must submit your request for relief within three years after the date the original tax return was filed or within two years after the date the tax was paid, whichever date is later. This period may be extended if you live in a presidentially declared disaster area, are affected by terrorist or military action, or are delayed by reason of an inability to manage your financial affairs because of physical or mental impairment.

A Combination of Balance Due and Refund/Credit

If you are requesting relief from a balance due as well as a refund or credit of amounts you have already paid, the time limits for refund or credit apply to the amounts you have already paid, and the time limits for a balance due will apply to any unpaid liability you have.

Relief from Liability for Tax Attributable to Item of Community Income (IRC Section 66(c))

In a community property state, generally speaking, the income of each spouse belongs equally to both spouses. No matter who earns the income, it belongs to the "marital estate," which is equally owned by both spouses. If a joint return is filed, this section does not apply. However, the nature of community income creates a unique issue when you and your spouse file separate returns in a community property state. Relief under this section exists to provide help to you if you file a separate return without knowledge of community income attributable to your spouse. For that reason, there are special rules for innocent spouse relief when you and your spouse file separate returns in a community property state. In order to obtain relief under these circumstances, the "Traditional Relief Conditions" must be met:[134]

Traditional Relief Conditions

1. You did not file a joint return for the year.

2. You omitted community income in your gross income when you filed your return.

3. The item of omitted community income is:

   a. Wages, salaries, and other compensation your spouse or former spouse received for services he or she performed as an employee.

   b. Income your spouse or former spouse derived from a trade or business he or she operated as a sole proprietor.

   c. Your spouse's or former spouse's distributive share of partnership income.

   d. Income from your spouse's (or former) separate property.

   e. Any other income that belongs to your spouse or former spouse under community property law.

4. You establish that you did not know of, and had no reason to know of, that community income.

    a. You did not actually know of the community income; or

    b. A reasonable person in similar circumstances would not have known of the items of community income.

5. Under all facts and circumstances, it would not be fair to include the item of community income in your gross income. Factors the IRS will consider:

    a. Whether you received a benefit, directly or indirectly, from the omitted item of community income;

    b. Whether your spouse deserted you.

    c. Whether you and your spouse have been divorced or separated.

Do You Qualify for Equitable Relief?

It is very difficult for you to establish that you did not know of or have reason to know of such community income. If you are unable to establish this element, the IRS may still grant equitable relief. If relief cannot be granted due to failure of one of the Traditional Relief Conditions, the IRS must consider the equitable relief factors of Section 4.03 of Revenue Procedure 2013-34.

Prior to considering the equitable relief factors, you must meet the following threshold requirements:[135]

Threshold Requirements for Equitable Relief Factors

*   You must apply for relief while the collection or refund statutes remain open. The collection statute (CSED) is generally 10 years from the date of assessment. The refund statute is generally three years from filing your return or two years from payment of the tax, whichever is later.

*   No assets were transferred between you and your spouse as part of a fraudulent scheme.

*   Your spouse did not transfer disqualified assets to you. A disqualified asset is any property transferred to you from your spouse in order to avoid tax or payment of tax. If disqualified assets were transferred, relief can only be granted to the extent the income tax liability exceeds the value of those assets.

*   You did not knowingly participate in the filing of a fraudulent return.

- The income tax liability from which you seek relief must be attributable to an erroneous item of income or erroneous deduction of your spouse, unless an exception applies.[136]

If you meet the threshold requirements, the IRS will consider the equitable relief factors listed in Revenue Procedure 2013-34. The factors are designed as guides and do not exclude other factors that may be present. The weight given to any factor depends on all the facts and circumstances of the case. The factors are as follows:[137]

Equitable Relief Factors

1. **Marital Status**. This factor weighs in favor of relief if you and your spouse are no longer married, are legally separated, widowed, or have not been members of the same household for the previous 12 months.

2. **Economic Hardship**. If denying relief will cause you to suffer economic hardship, this factor will weigh in favor of relief. The IRS will consider your income, expenses, and assets to determine if economic hardship exists.

3. **Knowledge or Reason to Know**. This factor will weigh in favor of relief if you did not know or have reason to know of the item giving rise to the understatement at the time you filed your return. If you had actual knowledge or reason to know of the item, this factor will weigh against relief.

4. **Legal Obligation**. If your spouse has the sole legal obligation to pay the outstanding income tax liability pursuant to a divorce decree or agreement, this factor will weigh in favor of relief. If you had the sole legal obligation, this factor will weigh against relief.

5. **Significant Benefit**. This factor will weigh against relief if you enjoyed significant benefits (beyond normal support) such as living a lavish lifestyle, owning luxury assets, or taking expensive vacations. If you enjoyed little to no benefit and only your spouse significantly benefited, this factor will weigh in favor of relief.

6. **Compliance with Tax Laws**. This factor relates to your good faith effort to comply with the income tax laws in the taxable years following the period for which relief is requested.
   a. This factor will weigh in favor of relief if you:
      i. Are compliant for taxable years after being divorced from your spouse; or

ii.   Remain married to your spouse, but file separate returns and are compliant with the tax laws.

    b.   This factor will weigh against relief if you:

       i.   Are not compliant for taxable years after being divorced from your spouse; or

      ii.   Remain married (whether or not legally separated or living apart) and continue to file joint returns after requesting relief and the returns are not compliant; or

     iii.   Remain married to your spouse, file separate returns, and are noncompliant with the tax laws.

7.   **Mental or Physical Health**. This factor would weigh in favor of relief if you were in poor mental or physical health at the time you filed the returns or at the time you requested relief. The IRS will consider the nature, extent, and duration of the condition.

8.   **Other Factors**. Other relevant factors on relief shall be considered.

How to Apply and Time Limits for Requesting Relief

Generally speaking, once you file your income tax return, the IRS has three years to assess additional taxes. If filing for relief from liability for tax attributable to an item of community income, you must file *Form 8857, Request for Innocent Spouse Relief* no later than six months before the expiration of the time period for assessment (including extensions) against your spouse for the tax year for which you are requesting relief. If, however, the IRS begins an examination during the last six months, you have 30 days to file the form following the IRS initial contact letter to you.

What If the IRS Denies Your Claim for Innocent Spouse Relief?

If you request innocent spouse relief and the IRS denies your claim, you still have options. In this case, you will need to appeal the finding.

How to Appeal an Adverse Finding

- Innocent Spouse Relief (IRC 6015(b))
- Innocent Spouse Relief - Separation of Liability Relief (IRC 61015(c))

- Innocent Spouse Relief - Equitable Relief (IRC 6015(f))

- Relief from Liability Attributable to Item of Community Income (IRC 66(c))

After the IRS has reviewed your request for the above types of relief, they will issue a Preliminary Determination Letter explaining their decision and the reasoning behind their decision. If you were denied the relief you requested, you have 30 days to appeal. Your appeal should be submitted on *Form 12509 Innocent Spouse Statement of Disagreement.* The form asks for identifying information and tax years involved and has a large blank space for you to enter your reasons for disagreement. Present your information in chronological order and give specific dates. Attach any supporting documentation and send the form and supporting documents to the office that sent the Preliminary Determination Letter.[138]

After reviewing your case, the IRS will send you a Final Determination Letter. Except in the case of a *Request for Relief from Liability Attributable to Item of Community Income* (IRC 66(c)),[139] if you disagree with the findings in the Final Determination Letter you can petition the Tax Court for relief. This must be done within 90 days from the date of the Final Determination Letter. You may also petition the Tax Court if the IRS has not issued a final determination letter within six months after you filed your initial request for relief.

NOTE: If the IRS has sent you a notice that qualifies you for a Collection Due Process hearing, you can request innocent spouse relief when you submit your *Form 12153, Request for a Collection Due Process or Equivalent Hearing* by requesting innocent spouse relief and attaching a completed *Form 8857, Request for Innocent Spouse Relief.*[140] You cannot raise innocent spouse relief under a Collection Due Process or Equivalent Hearing if the IRS has already made a final innocent spouse relief determination in a final determination letter or statutory notice of deficiency or if the Tax Court has entered a decision on the innocent spouse relief issue.[141]

Effect on Collection Statute Expiration Date

If you request relief under IRC 6015(b), 6015(c), or 6015(f), the collection period is suspended until a waiver is filed or until the expiration of the 90 days for petitioning the Tax Court. If you file a Tax Court Petition, the CSED is extended for the period of time it takes until the Tax Court decision becomes final under IRC Section 7481 plus 60 days in each instance.[142]

How to Complete Form 8857, Request for Innocent Spouse Relief

The Innocent Spouse provisions are complex, and the form you will use to request relief is six pages long and requests quite a bit of information so the IRS can determine which provision fits your circumstances. Fortunately, the IRS breaks down the request into bite-sized, comparatively simple questions. Gathering the following information (as it applies to you) will help you answer the questions on the form:

- Tax years for which you are requesting relief.

- Identification of spouse/former spouse.

- Marital status.

- Copies of death certificate, will, and divorce documents, as applicable.

- Your level of education and health/mental health considerations.

- Your knowledge/participation regarding finances, tax returns, and balances due.

- Large purchases/expenses and transfer of any assets to you.

- Assets, liabilities, monthly income, and expenses.

- Any domestic violence issues along with supporting documents/evidence.

- Additional information you want the IRS to consider in determining if it would be unfair to hold you liable for the tax.

IRS Forms and Publications Related to This Chapter:

- *Publication 971 – Innocent Spouse Relief*

- *Form 8857 – Request for Innocent Spouse Relief (and instructions for Form 8857)*

- *Publication 1660 – Collection Appeal Rights*

- *Form 9423 – Collection Appeal Request*

- *Form 12153 – Request for Collection Due Process or Equivalent Hearing*

- *Form 433-F – Collection Information Statement*

- *Form 12509 Innocent Spouse Statement of Disagreement*

CHAPTER 14:

Injured Spouse Allocation

Did the IRS take your portion of a joint overpayment to pay your spouse's past-due debt? If so, you may qualify as an Injured Spouse.

Generally speaking, if there is an overpayment of tax, the IRS will first apply the overpayment to any outstanding federal tax liability of the taxpayer. After any such application, the IRS is required to offset any remaining overpayment to satisfy certain unpaid debts, including:[143]

- Past due child support.

- Past due non-tax debt owed to federal agencies (such as student loans).

- Past-due legally enforceable state income tax obligations owed to a state.

- Past due unemployment compensation obligations.

If you file a joint return with your spouse and your spouse owes one of the above-referenced debts, the IRS will appropriate up to the entire joint refund to the payment of such debts. If you did not owe the debt, but your refund was taken, you are an "Injured Spouse."

Required Conditions

You do have recourse and can file *Form 8379, Injured Spouse Allocation,* to recover your share of the refund. To be eligible, the following conditions must exist (the form itself will walk you through these requirements):

- You must have filed a joint return.

- The IRS has or will apply the joint overpayment to one of the following past-due debts owed by your spouse:
  - Federal tax
  - State income tax
  - State unemployment compensation.
  - Child support
  - Spousal support
  - Federal non-tax debt (such as a student loan).
- You must not be legally obligated to pay the debt.
- <u>One</u> of these additional conditions must exist:
  - You live in a community property state (AZ, CA, ID, LA, NV, NM, TX, WA, and WI).
  - You made tax payments such as income tax withholding or estimated tax payments.
  - You had earned income, such as wages, salary, or self-employment income.
  - You did or will claim the earned income credit or additional child tax credit.
  - You did or will claim a refundable tax credit.

The form will also have you allocate income, deductions, and credits.

When to File Form 8379

You should file *Form 8379, Injured Spouse Allocation* when you become aware that all or part of your share of the overpayment was, or is expected to be, applied against your spouse's past-due obligation. You must file the form within three years from the due date of the original return (including extensions, if any) or within two years from the date the tax was paid that was later offset, whichever is later (some limited conditions will extend this time under Section 6511 of the Internal Revenue Code).

How to File Form 8379

If you believe your refund will be allocated to your spouse's debt, you can file the form with your income tax return. If so, you should write "INJURED SPOUSE" in the upper left corner of the first page of your joint return. You can also file this form separately. If you do so, be sure to attach copies of all *Forms W-2, W-2G,* and *1099.*

The IRS will calculate the portion of your refund (as opposed to your spouse's refund). If you file *Form 8379, Injured Spouse Allocation* with your tax return, you will receive your refund without offset. If you submit the form after your tax return has been processed, your portion of the refund will be calculated and returned to you.

If the IRS denies your application for injured spouse allocation, you will have 30 days to appeal their decision.

IRS Forms and Publications Related to This Chapter:

- *Form 8379 – Injured Spouse Allocation (and instructions for Form 8379)*
- *Publication 1660 – Collection Appeal Rights*

CHAPTER 15:

Appeals

In most cases, if the IRS denies your request or proposes to take an action against you or takes action against you, you can use the administrative appeal process. The IRS Independent Office of Appeals (commonly referred to as "Appeals") is an independent branch within the IRS that handles disputes between the IRS and taxpayers. This structure has benefits for both the IRS and the taxpayer. The appeals process is informal and, in most cases, can be handled via correspondence or telephone conference. The appeals function is to resolve tax disputes in a manner that is fair to both you and the IRS and to prevent unnecessary litigation. If the IRS is being a bit overzealous, if their collection action is in error, or if you have a collection alternative that will work, the appeals process might work in your favor.

If you appeal an action by the IRS, your case will be assigned to an Appeals Officer. While the goal of the collections representative is to enforce the collection of unpaid taxes, the goal of the Appeals Officer is to facilitate a resolution that is fair to you and the government. Once your appeal has been submitted, you will be contacted by the Appeals Officer, who will take a fresh, independent look at your case. You are allowed to present your side of the case, present any documents or information you have in support of your position, and, in many cases, present collection alternatives that are better suited to your circumstances.

In all my dealings with Appeals, I have found them to be professional and fair to the taxpayer. In many cases, they are more flexible than the collections personnel originally assigned to the case. You should not hesitate to appeal a matter that you believe to be unfair or overly harsh.

The two main appeals programs available in collections cases are the Collection Due Process Program (CDP) and the Collections Appeals Program (CAP).

Collection Due Process Program ("CDP")

This program is available to you if you have received one of the following notices:

- Notice of Federal Tax Lien Filing and Your Right to a Hearing under IRC 6320
- Final Notice - Notice of Intent to Levy and Notice of Your Right to a Hearing
- Notice of Jeopardy Levy and Right of Appeal
- Notice of Levy on Your State Tax Refund - Notice of Your Right to a Hearing
- Post-Levy Collection Due Process Notice

To appeal in these cases, complete *Form 12153, Request for a Collection Due Process or Equivalent Hearing.* You generally have 30 days to submit your appeal to the address shown on the lien or levy notice. The notice will also indicate the last day to file the appeal. Make sure the appeal is postmarked within the prescribed time. It is good practice to have proof of mailing (e.g., Certified Mail). If you miss the deadline, you can file for an "Equivalent Hearing" within one year of the original notice date.[144]

Completing Form 12153

Section 1: Check the box indicating the basis for the appeal. Check the box for Filed Notice of Federal Tax Lien or Notice of Proposed or Actual Levy as appropriate. Check both boxes if both apply.

Section 2: Check the box for an Equivalent Hearing if you have missed your deadline to file the CDP. An Equivalent Hearing will allow you to present your case to Appeals, but collection action will not be automatically stopped as it would for a non-equivalent CDP and you will not have the opportunity for a review of the findings in Tax Court. With an equivalent hearing, the CSED (Collection Statute Expiration Date) will not be extended.

Sections 3-6: Your information

Section 7: It is best to include a copy of your notice with *Form 12153*. However, you may enter the relevant information in Section 7 instead of including a copy of the notice.

Section 8: This section provides the reason you are requesting the hearing. Check all boxes that apply. The reasons include:

- You are not liable for the tax.

- You claim innocent spouse relief.

- Your taxes were discharged in bankruptcy.

- Payments you made were not properly applied.

- You are requesting the Notice of Federal Tax Lien be withdrawn.

- Financial hardship prevents payment.

- You would like a collection alternative.

- There is a space to include other issues or comments.

Section 9: If, in Section 8, you checked the box indicating you have a financial hardship or would like to propose a collection alternative, check the appropriate box in Section 9. Although not required, it will expedite the appeal if you include a financial statement (*Form 433-A* or *Form 433-B* for business).

Advantages of the CDP Program

- An impartial Settlement Officer who has not been involved in your case will conduct the hearing. This means you will receive an impartial review of your circumstances.

- Collection efforts are suspended until the case is resolved, so no new enforced collection efforts should take place (not applicable to equivalent hearings).

- You have the ability to have the Tax Court review the findings if they are not in your favor (not applicable to equivalent hearings).

Disadvantages of the CDP Program

- This appeal program is limited to specific types of collection cases.

- The Collections Statute Expiration Date (CSED) is extended until your case is finalized.

Collection Appeals Program ("CAP")

The Collection Appeals Program is available for the following actions:[145]

- Before or after the IRS files a Notice of Federal Tax Lien.

- A levy or seizure has occurred or is proposed.

- The filing of a notice of lien against an alter-ego or nominee's property.

- Denials of request to issue lien certificates, such as subordination, discharge, or non-attachment, as well as denials of requests to withdraw a Notice of Federal Tax Lien.

- Disallowance of your request to return levied property where:[146]

  - Levy not issued according to administrative procedures;

  - You have entered into an Installment Agreement;

  - The return of property would facilitate the collection of the tax;

  - The return of the property would be in the best interest of the taxpayer and government.

- Disallowance of property owner's claim for return of property taken under a wrongful levy[147] under IRC 6343(b).

- Termination or proposed termination of an Installment Agreement.

- Rejection of an Installment Agreement.

- Modification, or proposed modification, of an Installment Agreement.

How to Appeal Using the Collection Appeals Program

The procedures for this program are different from those of the CDP (Collection Due Process program).

First, if you disagree with the decision of an IRS employee regarding collections (excluding Installment Agreement issues), you must:

1. Request a conference with the employee's manager. Earlier is better, but generally, there is no deadline for requesting a CAP appeal.[148] However, undue delays may prejudice you in certain cases. **Exception**: If this is an appeal following a seizure, you only have ten days to contact the collection manager after the Notice of Seizure is provided to you or left at your home or place of business.

2. If you cannot resolve the issue with the collections manager, you must notify the collection office that you plan on submitting an appeal on *Form 9423, Collection Appeal Request,* within two business days after speaking with the collections manager.

3. The completed *Form 9423* must then be received or postmarked within three business days of the conference with the collection manager. Failure to follow these procedures may result in collection

action resuming. *Form 9423* must be submitted to the collection office involved in the action you are appealing.

If you request a conference with the collection manager and are not contacted within two business days, you can attempt to contact collections again, or you can submit *Form 9423*. If you submit *Form 9423*:

1. Note the date of your request for a conference in section 15 of the form and state that you were not contacted by a manager.

2. *Form 9423* must be received or postmarked within four business days of your request for a conference or collection action may resume. *Form 9423* must be submitted to the collection office involved in the action you are appealing.

Note: If you file *Form 9423, Collection Appeal Request* before a manager conference, the IRS will treat the form as a request for a manager conference and contact you within two workdays.

Special Rules for Installment Agreements

If your appeal is regarding an Installment Agreement that has been rejected, proposed for modification or modified, or proposed for termination or terminated, take the following action:

1. Complete and sign *Form 9423, Collection Appeal Request.*

2. Submit the form to the office or revenue officer who took the action regarding your Installment Agreement within 30 calendar days.

3. You are allowed, but not required, to request a manager conference to resolve the case before an appeal.

Completing Form 9423

Sections 1-10: Your information

Sections 11-13: Request information on the type of tax form, tax periods, and tax due.

Section 14: Check the box indicating which collection action you are appealing.

Section 15: In this section, you explain why you disagree with the collection actions you checked in section 14 and explain how you would resolve your tax problem. For example, if the collection action will cause you significant financial hardship, include this statement in Section 15. You should include your proposed collection alternative in this section as well. For instance, you might request to be placed in Currently Not Collectible status or propose different Installment Agreement terms that would not impose an undue hardship.

Advantages of CAP

- Available for a wider range of collection issues than are available for CDP hearings.
- An impartial Settlement Officer who has not been involved in your case will conduct the hearing. This means you will receive an impartial review of your circumstances.
- Participating in this program does not extend the Collection Statute Expiration Date (CSED).

Disadvantages of CAP

- Adverse findings cannot be reviewed by the Tax Court
- In some cases, qualification can be cumbersome due to the requirement to speak with the collection manager and short time periods for compliance.
- Collection actions are not automatically suspended. However, the IRS may suspend collection efforts based on your circumstances.

IRS Forms and Publications Related to This Chapter:

- *Publication 5 – Your Appeal Rights and How to Prepare a Protest if You Disagree*
- *Publication 1660 – Collection Appeal Rights*
- *Form 9423 – Collection Appeal Request*
- *Form 12153 – Request for Collection Due Process or Equivalent Hearing*
- *Form 433-F – Collection Information Statement*

CHAPTER 16:

Loss/Restriction of Your Passport

Has the IRS threatened to revoke or restrict your passport? Here is what you need to know.

Among the collection tools the IRS has is the threat of revocation of your passport if your account is seriously delinquent. Under the Fixing America's Surface Transportation (FAST) Act passed in 2015, the IRS can certify seriously delinquent tax debt to the U.S. Department of State, which may result in the denial, revocation, or limitation of a taxpayer's passport.[149]

What Constitutes "Seriously Delinquent Tax Debt?"

There are three requirements for a tax debt to be considered a Seriously Delinquent Tax Debt:

1. Federal tax debt, including assessed penalties and interest, that exceeds $62,000;[150] and

2. A Notice of Federal Tax Lien has been filed, and the time for appeal has lapsed, or the administrative appeals have been exhausted;[151] or

3. A levy has been issued.[152]

Restricting your passport is a severe measure, but there are exceptions contained in the Internal Revenue Code[153] and in the Internal Revenue Manual[154] that exempt most people who are trying to resolve their tax debt. If one of these exceptions applies to you, your case should not be certified to the U.S. Department of State. These exceptions include both statutory exclusions (contained in the Internal Revenue Code) and discretionary exclusions (exclusions provided by IRS policy):[155]

1. The debt is being paid in a timely manner as part of an Installment Agreement.[156]

2. The debt is being paid in a timely manner as part of an Offer in Compromise that has been accepted by the IRS.

3. The debt is being paid in a timely manner as part of a settlement agreement entered into with the Department of Justice.

4. The debt is subject to a levy for which collection has been suspended pending a Collection Due Process Hearing.

5. The debt collection has been suspended due to a claim for Innocent Spouse Relief.

6. If you are serving in a combat zone, certification is postponed.[157]

7. The debt is considered Currently Not Collectible due to hardship.

8. The debt resulted from identity theft.

9. You are in bankruptcy.

10. The debt is in a pending Offer in Compromise (you have submitted an OIC, but it has not yet been accepted by the IRS).

11. Debt is included in a pending Installment Agreement.

12. The debt has a pending adjustment that will fully pay the tax period.

It's important to note that the IRS will generally provide notice and an opportunity to resolve the tax debt before taking action against your passport.

What to do if the IRS has Already Certified Your Case to the State Department

If the IRS has already certified your account as a Seriously Delinquent Tax Debt, you may be able to have it reversed. A previously certified debt ceases to be a seriously delinquent tax debt when a statutory or discretionary exclusion is met.[158] In order to reverse a certification, the following must occur:

1. The tax debt is <u>paid in full</u>. A partial payment that brings the balance to less than the threshold to certify your debt ($62,000 in 2024) will not reverse the certification.[159]

2. The tax debt becomes legally unenforceable. For example, if the CSED has expired.

3. The tax debt ceases to be classified as a seriously delinquent tax debt. This occurs if one of the following exclusions apply:

   a. The debt is being paid in a timely manner as part of an Installment Agreement.

b. The debt is being paid in a timely manner as part of an Offer in Compromise that has been accepted by the IRS.

c. The debt is being paid in a timely manner as part of a settlement agreement entered into with the Department of Justice.

d. The debt is subject to a levy for which collection has been suspended pending a Collection Due Process Hearing.

e. The debt collection has been suspended due to a claim for Innocent Spouse Relief.

f. If you are a member of the armed forces and enter a combat zone, certification is reversed.[160]

g. The debt is considered Currently Not Collectible due to hardship.

h. The debt resulted from identity theft.

i. You are in bankruptcy.

j. The debt is in a pending Offer in Compromise (you have submitted an OIC, but it has not yet been accepted by the IRS).

k. Debt is included in a pending Installment Agreement.

l. The debt has a pending adjustment that will fully pay the tax period.

Once your debt is no longer classified as a seriously delinquent tax debt, the IRS will reverse the certification and notify the State Department within 30 days.

Getting Help from the IRS Regarding a Passport Certification Issue

If you have a question regarding your Passport Certification, you can call the dedicated IRS Passport Certification line at 855-519-4965. The representatives can answer your questions and provide assistance, including expedited certification reversals if you have planned international travel and have met the other requirements of certification reversal.

How to Appeal a Passport Certification

If you believe your Passport Certification is in error, unlike other collections activities, there is no administrative appeal process.[161] You may, however, bring a civil action against the United States in the Tax

Court or District Court. In order to avoid the expense and risks of litigation, it is best to address any Passport Certification issues as early as possible or take actions to meet certification reversal requirements.

CHAPTER 17:

Collection Statute Expiration Date (CSED)

Do you have some ancient tax debt? At some point, it may completely disappear.

The Collection Statute Expiration Date (CSED) marks the end of the period during which the IRS can collect taxes. This statute provides that the period for collection after assessing a tax liability is ten years.[162] With some exceptions, your tax debt will be forgiven if it is over ten years old. If you are interested in the CSED for a particular tax year, call the IRS. Their computer system tracks the CSED and calculates any extensions to the CSED. They have an up-to-date CSED for each of your tax years.

Extending the CSED

Be careful: Your actions can extend the time the IRS has to collect taxes. Certain actions, especially those that limit or suspend the IRS's ability to collect, will extend the Collection Statute Expiration Date (CSED). As your CSED approaches, carefully consider the implications of taking any of the following actions that will extend it:

1. **Offer in Compromise (OIC).** Filing an OIC will extend the CSED by the amount of time it is pending, plus 30 days. The IRS can take six to twelve months or more to investigate an OIC, and if it is accepted, the IRS will allow you up to two years to pay the settlement amount. Submitting an OIC is not always in your best interest.

2. **Collection Due Process appeal.** If you file *Form 12153, Request for a Collection Due Process or Equivalent* Hearing, your CSED will be extended while your hearing is pending until the request is withdrawn or the determination of Appeals becomes final. (Unless it is an Equivalent Hearing).

A possible strategy: If the CSED is close, you may consider filing a late-filed Collection Due Process appeal (filed after the 30-day Collection Due Process appeal period). It can be heard as an Equivalent Hearing. An Equivalent Hearing does not extend the CSED (it also does not prohibit levies). To qualify, the Equivalent Hearing must be filed within one year from the date of the CDP levy notice or one year plus five business days from the filing date of the NFTL.[163]

3. **Bankruptcy**. Bankruptcy extends the CSED by the time you were in bankruptcy, plus six months. If you filed for bankruptcy but did not eliminate all of your tax liabilities, the IRS will have more time to collect the non-discharged taxes from you.[164]

4. **Requesting Innocent Spouse Relief**. The collection period is suspended from filing the request for Innocent Spouse Relief until the 90-day period for petitioning the Tax Court expires. If a Tax Court petition is filed on an IRS denial, time is tolled (extended) until the Tax Court decision becomes final, plus 60 days.[165]

5. **Taxpayer Assistance Order** (*Form 911*). Suppose you are in a position necessitating the filing of *Form 911 (Application for Taxpayer Assistance Order)*. In that case, such filing will suspend the statute of limitations on collection while your case is pending review.[166]

6. **Installment Agreements**. The CSED is extended while your Installment Agreement is under consideration and for 30 days after a rejection of an Installment Agreement. A default or termination of your Installment Agreement will extend the CSED for 30 days. If the IRS refuses or defaults your Installment Agreement, you can appeal that decision. If you do, the collection statute is extended during the appeal.[167] Your CSED is not extended by virtue of an active Installment Agreement.

This list covers the most common events that affect your CSED, but it is not exhaustive. The common theme is that when a statute or policy prevents the IRS from collecting, the CSED is extended for the duration of that prevention. The IRS gains more time because these actions halt their ability to collect from you. Essentially, the relief from enforced collection activity that the IRS grants you is compensated by extending the CSED. Before proceeding, ensure that the potential for success (e.g., high chance of offer acceptance) is greater than the risk of extending the CSED and making your problem linger.

CHAPTER 18:

Taxpayer Advocate Service

A re you having a problem resolving an issue with the IRS? Are they taking forever to address your problem or request? Is the IRS causing financial hardship? The Taxpayer Advocate Service might be your answer.

- What is the Taxpayer Advocate Service?
- How do you contact the Taxpayer Advocate Service?
- What types of cases can the Taxpayer Advocate Service help with?

The Taxpayer Advocate Service (TAS) is an independent organization within the IRS that assists taxpayers who are experiencing financial difficulties or who are having problems resolving tax issues through normal IRS channels. TAS has offices in all 50 states, including the District of Columbia and Puerto Rico.

To contact TAS, you can:

1. Call the TAS toll-free hotline: The TAS hotline is available Monday through Friday, from 8:00 a.m. to 8:00 p.m. local time. The phone number for the TAS hotline is 1-877-777-4778.

2. Submit a request for assistance online: You can submit an electronic request for assistance through the TAS website at **www.TaxpayerAdvocate.IRS.gov**. The online request form will ask you to provide basic information about your tax issue, and you will need to provide your contact information.

3. Contact your local TAS office: You can find the address, phone number, and other contact information for your local TAS office on the TAS website, **www.TaxpayerAdvocate.IRS.gov**

It's important to note that the TAS is not a substitute for normal IRS procedures. You should try to resolve any tax issues through normal IRS channels before contacting the TAS. However, if you have already tried to resolve your issue through normal channels and have not been successful, or if you are experiencing financial difficulties, the TAS may be able to assist you in resolving your tax issues.

There are two categories of tax issues that the Taxpayer Assistance Office can help you resolve:

Financial Hardship

The Taxpayer Advocate Service can assist you if the IRS's actions will lead to economic harm. If you can answer yes to the following questions, you would qualify under the Financial Hardship category:

- Will you lose or not be able to remain in your house, not be able to get food, pay your utilities, or keep your transportation to work?

- Will you incur significant costs, such as fees for obtaining representation to help with relief?

- Will you suffer negative impacts such as loss of income, credit report damage, or any damage that cannot be restored to the way they were prior?

IRS Systems/Procedures Problem

The Taxpayer Advocate Service can help you if you are having problems with an IRS system or procedure, including:

- A delay of over 30 days beyond regular processing times to resolve a tax-related problem. These cases also occur when the IRS sends multiple interim responses (letters stating that the IRS will need more time to address your account issue) and the IRS takes no other actions to resolve your issues.

- If the IRS was supposed to respond to you or resolve your account by a specific date and they have not.

- An IRS system or procedure has failed to operate as intended or failed to resolve your problem or dispute with the IRS.

I recently used the TAS to help a widow whose deceased husband's tax refund was delayed. I called the IRS and was told it was "in process" and that I should call back in six weeks. In six weeks, I called back and was told it was still "in process" and to call back in another six weeks. After explaining the financial hardship this was causing, the agent merely stated that I would have to wait an additional six weeks and call back for an update. Clearly, the "normal channels" of the IRS were not handling my client's problem. I called the TAS, and they opened a case. The representative was able to track down the problem and have the refund issued promptly.

The Taxpayer Advocate has an "online qualifier" to help you determine if the TAS will be able to assist you. It is located at **https://www.taxpayeradvocate.irs.gov/can-tas-help-me-with-my-tax-issue/**

IRS Forms and Publications Related to This Chapter:

- *Publication 1546 – Taxpayer Advocate Service – Your Voice at the IRS*
- *Form 911- Request for Taxpayer Advocate Service Assistance*

CHAPTER 19:

Disaster-Related Suspension of Collections

The IRS may issue a collection hold or suspension of collection activities if you live in a disaster area. This means that the IRS will temporarily stop collection actions, such as liens, levies, and seizures if you are affected by a natural disaster or other significant event, such as a hurricane, earthquake, or pandemic.

To qualify for a disaster-related collection hold, you must live or have a business in an area designated by the Federal Emergency Management Agency (FEMA) as a major disaster area. The IRS will generally wait to resume collection activities until a reasonable time after the disaster has ended and taxpayers have has had time to recover.

It is important to note that while a disaster-related collection hold may temporarily suspend IRS collections, it does not eliminate or reduce the amount of tax debt owed. Once the hold is lifted, you will still be responsible for paying any taxes owed, including penalties and interest.

You can check if you are in a federally declared disaster area by visiting the IRS website's "Disaster Assistance and Emergency Relief for Individuals and Businesses" page at **www.IRS.gov/businesses/small-businesses-self-employed/disaster-assistance-and-emergency-relief-for-individuals-and-businesses**.
This page provides information on current disaster relief efforts, including any tax relief provisions that may be available to affected taxpayers. The website also includes information on contacting the IRS for further assistance.

PART IV: RESOURCES AND HELPFUL INFORMATION

CHAPTER 20:

Taxpayer Bill of Rights

In the not-so-distant past, legitimate worries surfaced regarding the IRS's disproportionate emphasis on enforcement at the expense of customer service and taxpayer rights. As a tax lawyer, I witnessed how this enforcement-centric approach colored interactions with the IRS. Driven by these concerns and an effort by the then National Taxpayer Advocate, the Taxpayer Bill of Rights was codified in 2015.[168] This legislation aimed to recalibrate the IRS's priorities, establishing a framework that safeguarded the service and due process rights of taxpayers navigating the agency's landscape. The IRS seeks to ensure that every taxpayer is treated with dignity, fairness, and respect in their interactions with the IRS.

Taxpayer Bill of Rights

The Right to Be Informed

Taxpayers have the right to receive clear and easily understandable information about their tax obligations, including how to comply with tax laws and what they can expect during the tax process.

The Right to Quality Service

Taxpayers have the right to receive prompt, courteous, and professional assistance from IRS employees when seeking help or interacting with the agency.

The Right to Pay No More than the Correct Amount of Tax

Taxpayers have the right to pay only the amount of tax legally owed, with accurate calculations, deductions, and credits applied to their tax liability.

The Right to Challenge the IRS's Position and Be Heard

Taxpayers have the right to question the IRS's decisions, provide evidence, and have their objections considered during the examination, appeal, and collection processes.

The Right to Appeal an IRS Decision in an Independent Forum

Taxpayers have the right to a fair and impartial administrative appeal of most IRS decisions, including the right to take their case to court.

The Right to Finality

Taxpayers have the right to know the maximum amount of time they have to challenge the IRS's position, as well as the timeframe for completing an audit or collection action.

The Right to Privacy

Taxpayers have the right to expect that any information they provide to the IRS will be kept confidential, within the limits of the law.

The Right to Confidentiality

Taxpayers have the right to expect that any information they provide to the IRS will not be disclosed to other parties unless authorized by the taxpayer or by law.

The Right to Retain Representation

Taxpayers have the right to retain an authorized representative, such as a tax professional, to represent them in their interactions with the IRS.

The Right to a Fair and Just Tax System

Taxpayers have the right to expect fairness, integrity, and impartiality from the IRS in its dealings with them.

These rights are intended to empower taxpayers and ensure a more balanced and transparent relationship between individuals and the IRS. The Taxpayer Bill of Rights serves as a reference point for taxpayers to understand their rights and hold the IRS accountable for its actions.

CHAPTER 21:

Other Resources

Professional assistance can be costly, but there are resources available for free or reduced cost.

Low-Income Taxpayer Clinics

Low-Income Taxpayer Clinics (LITCs) provide free or low-cost legal assistance to low-income taxpayers who have disputes with the IRS or need help to understand their tax rights and responsibilities. Here's some information about LITCs:

Services Provided

LITCs offer a range of services, including:

- Representing taxpayers in IRS audits, appeals, and collection disputes.

- Helping taxpayers respond to IRS notices and letters.

- Assisting with tax court proceedings.

- Educating taxpayers about their rights and responsibilities under the tax law.

Eligibility

LITCs generally serve individuals whose income is below a certain threshold and have limited English proficiency. Each clinic sets its own eligibility criteria, so it's best to check with the specific clinic in your area.

Locations

LITCs are located throughout the United States and its territories. You can find a current list of LITC in IRS Publication 4134 on the IRS website, by contacting your local IRS office, or calling the IRS at 800-829-1040.

Confidentiality

LITCs maintain strict confidentiality regarding their clients' information and communications.

Funding

LITCs receive funding from the IRS through grants, as well as from other sources such as state governments, bar associations, and nonprofit organizations.

If you need assistance with IRS-related issues and meet the income eligibility requirements, contacting a Low Income Taxpayer Clinic may be a valuable resource for you.

Community Tax Clinics

Many communities have community-based organizations, legal aid societies, or volunteer income tax assistance programs that offer free or low-cost tax assistance to taxpayers in need. Local bar associations are a trade group comprised of local attorneys. Calling your local bar association might yield a pro bono (free) attorney to help. The local bar association is also likely to know of any other local programs to assist taxpayers.

IRS Website

The IRS has a wealth of information on its site and now has the option for taxpayers to sign up for an online account. With an online account, taxpayers can:

- View balance
- Make and view payments
- View or create payment plans
- Manage communication preferences
- Access tax records
- View tax professional authorizations.

To establish an online account you will need to create and account with ID.me, a third party technology provider. There is a rather robust verification protocol, but having an online account is useful tool to access your account information. To establish an account, go to IRS.gov and click on the icon for "Sign in to your account." It will walk you through the process of establishing your online account.

IRS YouTube Channel

The IRS also has a YouTube channel with valuable information about many tax topics, including information for taxpayers who are facing collections challenges. The IRS channel is located at **www.YouTube.com/@irsvideos/videos.**

IRS Free File

The IRS just launched a program that provides taxpayers with an adjusted gross income of $79,000 or less the ability to use guided tax software (the program asks you questions and guides you through the filing process). This can be found at **www.IRS.gov/irs-free-file-do-your-taxes-for-free.**

CHAPTER 22:

Eleven Tips to Keep Your Case on Track

This list of strategies will keep you in good standing and prevent any unwanted collection events from the IRS:

Adjust your Withholding

You can adjust your withholding amounts to ensure you pay enough withholding to cover your tax obligation. This can help prevent a large tax bill at the end of the year. Contact your employer and complete a new *Form W-4, Employee's Withholding Certificate* to calculate the proper withholding amount. Not sure how much to withhold? Use the Tax Withholding Estimator at **www.IRS.gov/individuals/tax-withholding-estimator**.

Make Your Estimated Tax Payments

If you are self-employed or have other sources of income that are not subject to withholding, you may need to make estimated tax payments throughout the year. This can help prevent a large tax bill at the end of the year as well as prevent the imposition of underpayment penalties. See page 20 of IRS *Publication 505, Tax Withholding and Estimated Tax* for details on determining your estimated tax payment obligations.

File on Time

Filing tax returns on time can help prevent penalties and interest charges. If you cannot file on time, file for an extension using *Form 4868, Application for Automatic Extension of Time to File US Individual Income Tax Return*. This will provide an extension of time to file your return, but your taxes are still due by the due date. A common mistake is to delay filing your return because you know you owe money. If you file and don't pay, your penalties will be much less than if you neither file nor pay.

Keep Accurate Records

Keeping accurate records can help prevent mistakes and discrepancies with the IRS. Keeping accurate records can also help you claim deductions and credits that reduce tax liability. Each time you speak with an IRS representative, they will tell you their name and ID number. Keep a record of whom you speak with and the contents of the discussion.

Do Not Ignore IRS Notices

Read and respond to IRS notices. If a certified letter awaits you at the post office, go get it. Once the IRS mails the notice, they have complied with their statutory obligations. You gain no advantage by failing to read the notice.

If You Owe Money to the IRS, Call Them

Yes, their job is to collect money. However, it is also their job to help you resolve your case. They don't get a bonus for squeezing money out of you. If circumstances dictate, they would just as soon place you in a Currently Not Collectible status as they would set up an Installment Agreement for you.

Be Prepared When You Call

If you have time to prepare before calling the IRS, collect a recent pay-stub and pencil in a *Form 433-F Collection Information Statement*. Under most circumstances, this information will be sufficient to wrap up your case. If don't have time to prepare before you call the IRS, call them anyway. They will give you time to collect your financial data.

Don't Take Out Your Frustrations on the Representative

If you are nervous to make the call or nervous about the possible outcomes, tell the representative, "*Hey, I'm a bit nervous, I have never owed tax before and I don't know what to expect.*" That will get you much further than exhibiting anger.

Hold Up Your End of the Bargain

If you commit to getting back to the IRS with information, do so before the deadline. If you need more time, call back and ask. If you are making monthly payments, make them on time (or enter into a direct debit Installment Agreement so it is done automatically). If you cannot meet your commitment, call them and tell them. They will usually be able to give you some leeway.

Artificial Intelligence Warning

Everybody is using AI now. AI works well if you need to look up a form or find the address of your local IRS office. Do not use AI to answer critical questions regarding your case. AI operates by collecting all the data on the internet and coming up with an answer for you. As you know, not everything on the internet is correct. I have tested AI by inputting tax law questions. In most cases, the answers were incomplete or flat out wrong.

Don't Hide Your Assets

It can be tempting to conceal assets or provide inaccurate information when completing financial statements for your tax case. Doing so creates unnecessary risk. Not only does hiding assets jeopardize the integrity of your case, but it can also lead to severe consequences, including criminal prosecution.[169] Instead, prioritize transparency and honesty through the process. There are plenty of legitimate avenues and strategies available to navigate your case within the bounds of the law. By playing by the rules and providing accurate information, you can effectively resolve your case while mitigating unnecessary risks.

CONCLUSION

As you reach the final pages of this book, I want to commend you for taking control of your tax debt. Navigating the complexities of tax collections can be daunting, but armed with the knowledge and strategies shared throughout these chapters, you are well-equipped to face the challenges ahead. For the best results, do not procrastinate. Instead, maintain a proactive mindset and stay informed about your rights and options. With determination, diligence, and a commitment to resolving your tax issues, you have the power to overcome any obstacle and achieve an outcome that works for you.

Your dedication to taking control of your tax debt is a testament to your strength and resolve.

I wish you all the best in your endeavors, and may your path forward be paved with success and prosperity.

Warm regards,

Robert C. Platt

ENDNOTES

[1] There is an exception to general notice requirements if collection is in jeopardy

[2] Internal Revenue Code § 6502

[3] *Internal Revenue Manual* § 1.2.1.6.18

[4] These are government-wide identifications established by Homeland Security Presidential Directive 12

[5] Following Covid, these letters are generally sent eight weeks apart

[6] Determined by the last filed tax return or filing a Form 8822.

[7] Personal delivery is also allowed.

[8] *Internal Revenue Manual* § 5.11.4

[9] Internal Revenue Code § 6331(h)

[10] As of 2024. This amount is indexed for inflation.

[11] *Internal Revenue Manual* § 4.13.1.5

[12] *Internal Revenue Manual* § 20.1.1.3.2(1)

[13] *Internal Revenue Manual* § 20.1.1.3.2.2(1)

[14] *Internal Revenue Manual* § 20.1.1.3.2.2(2)(b)

[15] *Internal Revenue Manual* § 20.1.1.3.2.2(2)(c)

[16] *Internal Revenue Manual* § 20.1.1.3.2.2.3

[17] *Internal Revenue Manual* § 20.1.1.3.3.2.1

[18] Internal Revenue Code § 6159

[19] *Internal Revenue Service Data Book, 2023*, Table 27

[20] Internal Revenue Code § 6651(a)(2)

[21] *Internal Revenue Manual* § 5.14.1.2(7)

[22] Internal Revenue Code § 6331(k)(2)

[23] *Internal Revenue Manual* § 5.15.1.8

[24] Internal Revenue Code § 6159(c)

[25] *Internal Revenue Manual* § 5.14.1.2(2) and § 5.14.5.2(14)

[26] *Internal Revenue Manual* § 5.19.1.6.4

[27] Internal Revenue Code § 6159(a); *Internal Revenue Manual* § 5.14.2.1.1(2)

[28] *Internal Revenue Manual* § 5.14.2.2(2)

[29] *Internal Revenue Manual* § 5.14.2.2.2(3)

[30] Internal Revenue Code § 6502(a)(2)(a); *Internal Revenue Manual* § 5.14.2.3(1)

[31] *Internal Revenue Manual* § 5.14.10.2

[32] *Internal Revenue Manual* § 5.15.1.9(1) and (2)

[33] *Internal Revenue Manual* § 5.15.1.10.1

[34] These out of pocket standards are based on the Medical Expenditure Panel Survey and represent the average cost for consumers. By virtue of the definition of average, approximately half of the taxpayers will be expending more than this amount each month.

[35] *Internal Revenue Manual* § 5.14.1.4.2(2)

[36] *Internal Revenue Manual* § 5.14.11.5(5)

[37] In some PPIA, there will be an extension of the CSED.

[38] *Internal Revenue Manual* § 5.14.5.4

[39] *Internal Revenue Manual* § 5.14.7.2(1)(a)

[40] *Internal Revenue Manual* § 5.14.7.4(7)

[41] Internal Revenue Code § 6672

[42] Internal Revenue Code § 7122; 26 CFR § 301.7122-1; Rev. Proc. 2003-71

[43] *Internal Revenue Service Data Book, 2023*, Table 27

[44] *Internal Revenue Manual* § 5.8.1.2.2; Policy Statement 5-100 in *Internal Revenue Manual* § 1.2.1.6.17

[45] *Internal Revenue Manual* § 5.8.7.7.1 Not in the Best Interest of the Government Rejection

[46] Reasonable Collection Potential is net equity, plus future net income, and other components of collectibility (e.g. Collection Statute Expiration Date).

[47] *Internal Revenue Manual* § 5.8.5.25

[48] *Internal Revenue Manual* § 5.8.5.25(3)

[49] *Internal Revenue Manual* § 5.8.5.4.1

[50] *Internal Revenue Manual* § 5.8.5.25

[51] *Internal Revenue Manual* § 5.8.5.25(3)

[52] *Internal Revenue Manual* § 5.8.5.4.1

[53] *Internal Revenue Manual* § 5.8.5.22.1(3)

[54] IRS.gov/business/small-buisness-self-employed/collection-financial-standards

[55] *Internal Revenue Manual* § 5.8.5.4.1(1)

[56] *Internal Revenue Manual* § 5.8.5.4.1(3)

[57] *Internal Revenue Manual* § 5.8.5.7(1)

[58] *Internal Revenue Manual* § 5.8.5.8(3)

[59] *Internal Revenue Manual* § 5.8.5.11

[60] *Internal Revenue Manual* § 5.8.5.12(2)

[61] *Internal Revenue Manual* § 5.8.5.3

[62] *Internal Revenue Manual* § 5.8.12.1(1)

[63] Internal Revenue Code § 7122(e)

[64] *Internal Revenue Manual* § 5.8.4.2(3); 26 CFR § 301.7122-1(b)(3)

[65] *Internal Revenue Manual* § 5.8.4.2(4)

[66] *Internal Revenue Manual* § 5.8.11.3.2.1(2)

[67] *Internal Revenue Manual* § 5.8.11.3.2.1(3)

[68] *Internal Revenue Manual* § 5.8.11.3.2.1(4)

[69] *Internal Revenue Manual* § 5.8.11.3.2.1(5)

[70] *Internal Revenue Manual* § 5.8.11.3.2.1(9)

[71] *Internal Revenue Manual* § 5.8.11.3.2.1(10)

[72] *Internal Revenue Manual* § 5.8.11.3.2.1(12)

[73] See Form 843, Claim for Refund and Request for Abatement

[74] *Internal Revenue Manual* § 5.8.1.15(6)

[75] *Internal Revenue Manual* § 5.8.1.15(6)

[76] *Internal Revenue Manual* § 5.8.1.6.4

[77] *Internal Revenue Manual* § 5.8.11.2(5)

[78] *Internal Revenue Manual* § 5.8.11.5 (1)

[79] *Internal Revenue Manual* § 5.8.11.5.3

[80] *Internal Revenue Manual* § 5.8.11.3.2.1(2)

[81] *Internal Revenue Manual* § 5.8.11.3.2.1(3)

[82] *Internal Revenue Manual* § 5.8.11.3.2.1(4)

[83] *Internal Revenue Manual* § 5.8.11.3.2.1(5)

[84] *Internal Revenue Manual* § 5.8.11.3.2.1(9)

[85] *Internal Revenue Manual* § 5.8.11.3.2.1(10)

[86] *Internal Revenue Manual* § 5.8.11.3.2.1(12)

[87] *Internal Revenue Manual* § 5.8.11.2(6)

[88] *Internal Revenue Manual* § 5.8.11.2(5)

[89] *Internal Revenue Manual* § 5.8.12.1(1)

[90] Internal Revenue Code § 7122(e)

[91] 11 United States Code § 523

[92] *Internal Revenue Service Data Book, 2023,* Table 27

[93] There are some exceptions to the pre-levy notice requirements in *Internal Revenue Manual* § 5.11.1.3.2(7).

[94] *Internal Revenue Manual* § 5.11.1.3.2(4)

[95] Internal Revenue Code § 6334(a)

[96] Internal Revenue Code § 6334(d)

[97] Internal Revenue Code § 151(d)(5)

[98] The current iteration of Form 12153 actually has a web address to see if you can qualify for an Installment Agreement without submitting financial statements.

[99] Internal Revenue Code § 6343(a)

[100] *Internal Revenue Manual* § 5.16.1.2.9(12); *Internal Revenue Manual* § 5.11.1.3.1(2)

[101] If you fail to return the form to your employer you are treated as married filing separately with no dependents for purposes of the calculations.

[102] 26 C.F.R. § 301.6331-1(c)

[103] *Internal Revenue Manual* § 5.11.2.2.7(2)

[104] Internal Revenue Code § 6332(c)

[105] Internal Revenue Code § 6334(e)(1)(A)

[106] Internal Revenue Code § 6337

[107] Internal Revenue Code § 6331(d)(3)

[108] IRS Policy Statement 4-88; *Internal Revenue Manual* § 1.2.1.5.27; *Internal Revenue Manual* § 5.11.3.3

[109] Internal Revenue Code § 6867

[110] Internal Revenue Code § 7429(a)(1)(B)

[111] *Internal Revenue Service Data Book, 2023,* Table 27

[112] Internal Revenue Code § 6321; this is also called an "assessment lien."

[113] *Internal Revenue Manual* § 5.12.2.6

[114] *Internal Revenue Manual* § 5.12.2.3.1(1)

[115] https://www.experian.com/blogs/ask-experian/tax-liens-are-no-longer-a-part-of-credit-reports/

[116] See Revenue Ruling 68-57 and Publication 785

[117] Internal Revenue Code §6325(a)(1)

[118] Internal Revenue Code §6323(j)(1)

[119] See PMTA 2009-158 for detailed treatment of release vs. withdrawal.

[120] Internal Revenue Code § 6325(d)(1)

[121] Internal Revenue Code § 6325(d)(2)

[122] Internal Revenue Code § 6015; *Internal Revenue Manual* § 25.15

[123] Internal Revenue Code § 6015(b)(2)

[124] Treas. Reg. § 1.6015-3(c)(2)(v)

[125] Internal Revenue Code § 6015(c)(4)(B)

[126] Internal Revenue Code § 6015(f)

[127] *Internal Revenue Manual* § 25.15.3.9.3

[128] *Internal Revenue Manual* § 25.15.3.9.2.1

[129] *Internal Revenue Manual* § 25.15.3.8.2.6

[130] See *Internal Revenue Manual* § 25.15.3.9.2.1 for exceptions and calculations.

[131] *Internal Revenue Manual* § 25.15.3.9.3

[132] Rev. Proc. 2013-34; *Internal Revenue Manual* § 25.15.3.9.4.1

[133] There are exceptions to this rule if abuse or restricted access to financial information is present.

[134] *Internal Revenue Manual* § 25.15.5.14.1

[135] *Internal Revenue Manual* § 25.15.5.14.2

[136] *Internal Revenue Manual* § 25.15.3.9.2.1

[137] Rev. Proc. 2013-34; *Internal Revenue Manual* § 25.15.3.9.4.1

[138] IRS Publication 5 provides tips on how to prepare a protest if you disagree with the determination.

[139] See *Bernal v. Commissioner*, 120 T.C. 102 (2003) which held there is no standalone right to petition the tax court for denial of relief pursuant to Internal Revenue Code § 66(c).

[140] *Internal Revenue Manual* § 8.7.12.13(1); Form 12153 Instructions

[141] *Internal Revenue Manual* § 8.7.12.13(3); 26 CFR § 301.6330-1(e)

[142] *Internal Revenue Manual* § 8.21.5.5.7(2)

[143] Internal Revenue Code § 6402

[144] One year plus five days in the case of filing of a Notice of Federal Tax Lien.

[145] *Internal Revenue Manual* § 5.1.9.4(1)

[146] Internal Revenue Code § 6343(d)

[147] Internal Revenue Code § 6343(b)

[148] *Internal Revenue Manual* § 5.1.9.4.2(4)

[149] Internal Revenue Code § 7345

[150] As of 2024. This number is indexed for inflation.

[151] Internal Revenue Code § 6320

[152] *Internal Revenue Manual* § 5.19.25.3

[153] Internal Revenue Code § 7345(b)(2), Statutory Exclusions

[154] *Internal Revenue Manual* § 5.19.25.5, Discretionary Exclusions

[155] *Internal Revenue Manual* § 5.19.25.5; these are conditions under which the IRS has chosen to provide relief in addition to the statutory exclusions.

[156] Some short term payment plans and continuous wage levies are excluded from this exception, see *Internal Revenue Manual* § 5.19.25.4(?)

[157] *Internal Revenue Manual* § 5.19.25.4(1)(e)

[158] *Internal Revenue Manual* § 5.19.25.10(1)

[159] *Internal Revenue Manual* § 5.19.25.10(1)a.

[160] *Internal Revenue Manual* § 5.19.25.10(4)b.

[161] *Internal Revenue Manual* § 5.19.25.13

[162] Internal Revenue Code § 6502

[163] Treas. Reg. § 301.6330-1(g)(3), ex.1; *Internal Revenue Manual* § 5.1.9.3.6

[164] Internal Revenue Code § 6503(h); *Internal Revenue Manual* § 5.9.4.2

[165] Internal Revenue Code § 6015(e)(2); *Internal Revenue Manual* § 25.15.1.8

[166] Internal Revenue Code § 7811(d); *Internal Revenue Manual* § 13.1.14

[167] Internal Revenue Code § 6331(k)(2)(d)

[168] Internal Revenue Code § 7803(a)(3)

[169] Internal Revenue Code § 7206(4)

Made in United States
Orlando, FL
27 June 2025